totally bonsai

totally bonsai

A guide to growing, shaping, and caring for miniature trees and shrubs

Craig Coussins

TUTTLE PUBLISHING
Boston · Rutland, Vermont · Tokyo

A Quintet book

First published in the United States in 2001 by Tuttle Publishing, an imprint of Periplus Editions (HK) Ltd, with editorial offices at 153 Milk Street, Boston, Massachusetts 02109.

Library of Congress Cataloging-in-Publication Data in Process

ISBN 0 8048 3420 2

This book was conceived, designed and produced by
Quintet Publishing Limited
6 Blundell Street
London
N7 9BH

Creative Director: Richard Dewing
Managing Editors: Toria Leitch, Diana Steedman
Art Director: Sharanjit Dhol
Designer: DW Design
Photographer: Ian Howes

Distributed by
North America
Tuttle Publishing
Distribution Center
Airport Industrial Park
364 Innovation Drive
North Clarendon, VT 05759-9436
Tel: (802) 773-8930
Tel: (800) 526-2778
Fax: (802) 773-6993

Japan
Tuttle Publishing
RK Building, 2nd Floor
2-13-10 Shimo-Meguro, Meguro-Ku
Tokyo 153 0064
Tel: (81) 35-437-0171
Fax: (81) 35-437 0755

Asia Pacific
Berkely Books Pte Ltd
130 Joo Seng Road
#06-01/03
Olivine Building
Singapore 368357
Tel: (65) 280-3320
Fax: (65) 280-6290

First edition
06 05 04 03 02 01 10 9 8 7 6 5 4 3 2 1

Manufactured in Hong Kong
Printed in China

Dedication

For many years, I have been a great admirer of a very special person who has been an inspiration to everyone who has met him. He taught me that it is not only how clever your techniques are but also how well you can teach those techniques. His humor is legendary and every workshop he has hosted, critiques he has given, or demonstration he has conducted is not only memorable, but is always remarkable to those fortunate enough to be there.

From the time I spent with him during 1984 and many times since, I have tried to follow his unique ability to guide, motivate, and share. I would like to give grateful thanks to the most able, generous and honored bonsai teacher in the world. He is always in my heart whenever I work or teach bonsai.

This book is dedicated to John Yoshio Naka.

Contents

Preface

Salvatore Liporace *Studio Botanico, Milan, Italy*

This Japanese word *chowa* means mind, heart, and hands. These three things are what guide the bonsai enthusiast.

A long time ago, starving for knowledge, I followed the teachings of several instructors, acquiring useful information for the future. Among many I met on the path of knowledge was a Japanese master who deeply amazed me with the message he was able to give to his pupils.

This first visit was followed by a further short period in Italy, during which I would discover that, despite not being an artist, this master was able to teach bonsai in a special way. He managed to touch the soul of his pupils very deeply by underlining the spiritual relationship between man and tree.

Many years went by, yet I still remember with pleasure the short time spent following that master's lessons. He instilled in me such great enthusiasm that, despite not being my teacher, he left a deep awareness of chowa in me.

There grew in me the understanding that all the different teachers and their viewpoints on how to create a bonsai, although giving me a strong basis, could not completely satisfy my artistic hunger. I was ready to choose the Master whom I would accompany for the rest of my life, involving and charming me in his never-ending pursuit of renewal. It was a revitalization through experimentation. Never satisfied with his goals, he looked always beyond the horizon of his own abilities.

The beginner usually follows the teachings of many instructors, drawing from each of them different lessons and truths. It may be a confusing period but, conversely, this period of learning can enrich the soul and mind of the pupil, allowing him or her to compare many techniques and approaches to the art of bonsai.

This is, of course, a complicated world, where techniques and understanding fuse together in creative bonding. At this point students of bonsai start making sense of the rules they have learned. When they feel comfortable with these rules, the artistic juices start flowing. The acquiring of working methods and the discipline of learning these techniques with a number of different masters will prepare you for an all over artistic understanding.

Craig Coussins, in choosing to place side by side works of other masters and himself, allows the beginner to compare different methods and bonsai approaches. The other artists' work underline the author's generosity in that, without fearing comparison with the work of others, he has extended the horizon of knowledge to this noble art.

Congratulations to my friend Craig for his book, which I wish a great success, and many thanks for choosing some works from Studio Botanico.

About the Bonsai Artists

Salvatore Liporace is one of the top Bonsai Masters in Europe. A student of Masahiko Kimura, recognized as one of the top masters in the world, Master Liporace now travels the world teaching bonsai and runs the famous Studio Botanico in Milan, which offers regular classes for young masters and designers. His bonsai nursery just outside Milan is nearing completion as I write.

As well as Liporace's own work, I have featured work from one of his students, Luigi Maggione, who achieved distinction in the prestigious Ben Oki Awards run by Bonsai Clubs International, based in the United States. Luigi's work won the International Award in 2000.

I also show work from Masters in different countries. Koos le Roux is a Bonsai Master specializing in landscape planting. His exquisite works use the unique South African stone found in the Transvaal region. Koos emulates landscapes seen throughout Africa and especially in the Republic of South Africa where he lives.

Joe Day has a nursery in Alabama and runs regular classes for his students. Joe works with Box (*Buxus*), Trident maple (*Acer buergerianum*) and other locally grown material. He works in many styles and is particularly fond of group styles.

Gary Marchal is one of the USA's leading experts on Bald or Swamp Cypress (*Taxodium distichum*). He lives in New Orleans and has grown excellent mature Cypress as bonsai, and Mary Madison, one of America's leading exponents of Buttonwoods (*Conocarpus*).

Foreword

This book may not turn you into a bonsai expert but it is intended to help you understand what is needed to look after a bonsai. Later in the book I look at more advanced techniques, for I am sure you will agree you should be given the tools to allow you to either develop as an artist in bonsai or simply to find out a little more about this truly fascinating craft. It is such a wonderful hobby, because it comprises art, horticulture, and traditional Oriental discipline. It is a modern as well as an ancient art form, and everyone can enjoy the happiness of looking after a miniature tree.

And there we have the essence of it. Imagine the enormous redwood shrunk to a size that you can carry in one hand, but in perfect detail throughout? That is the joy of bonsai—bringing nature into your home or garden. I never tire of the wonder of seeing a perfect miniature tree, and that image immediately transports me far and away into the countryside or the mountains, in the time it takes to concentrate on the trunk and the shape.

I am not the first to say this and, after two thousand years of history, I can certainly state that I will not be the last. Bonsai and its Chinese equivalent, *penjing*, is an art form that is fast developing all over the world. It is no longer the sole preserve of the Far East but is now taught in villages, towns, and cities in every country in the world. Some of the finest experts are from Japan or China, but now just about everywhere can boast a local bonsai teacher or master. North America and Europe are particularly well served. No matter where you are, there are wonderful teachers ready to help you become proficient in making a bonsai tree.

Reading this book is a good start. It will help you onto the path of understanding. It should help you keep your bonsai alive and perhaps inspire you to find out more about this popular and fascinating hobby.

I have repeated care points throughout the book in order to emphasize their important aspects.

I would especially like to thank Salvatore Liporace for his generosity in allowing me access to his photo library.

Craig Coussins

About the Author

△ **Craig Coussins, with his wife Svetlana**

Craig Coussins started growing bonsai in 1973. He first saw a real bonsai in a window of a flower shop in 1972 and immediately started reading and looking for information.

The English bonsai teacher, Peter Adams taught him from 1977 through 1991. During 1984, he met John Yoshio Naka, the world-famous Japanese–American bonsai teacher. This was while he was on a tour he was organizing with the Federation of British Bonsai Societies, a body he helped to bring into being in 1982. Craig filmed *Sensei* (Teacher) Naka over five three-hour demonstrations. It was, as Craig said at the time, a unique way to get to know a bonsai master.

John Naka's enthusiasm inspired Craig to start teaching and he has been a regular teacher throughout the UK since that time. In 1992, Craig started teaching in other countries and has now visited Russia, South Africa, New Zealand, Ireland, California, Texas, Florida, Italy, and Belgium. Guest speaker at many international conventions around the world, Craig is a popular teacher in workshops, his favorite way of teaching his art.

He was the founder of the Scottish Bonsai Association in 1978 and a

◁ **John Yoshio Naka with his first tree**

founder committee member of the Federation of British Bonsai Societies in 1981. He is also a recipient of the Royal Caledonian Horticultural Society Neal Medal for services to Scottish horticulture through his work on the development of bonsai art in Scotland.

Craig likes forest-style bonsai, and his favorite species include maples, junipers, yews, elms, pines, and larch. He recently loaned his entire collection of bonsai, bonsai pots from important British ceramicists, and his collection of antique Chinese and Japanese bonsai pots to Peter Snart at Willowbog Bonsai in Keilder Forest, Northumbria, in northern England. Willowbog, a former farm, is a successful bonsai nursery.

Craig is also known for his collection of "viewing stones," or *suiseki*, which numbers over 1,000 pieces collected from around the world. *Suiseki* are collected for their beauty and resemblance to natural features such as landscapes and mountains, and are often used with bonsai as part of the display. Craig's collection is displayed at the bonsai workshop facility at Willowbog and is the core of the Bonsai Museum being built there. Craig is a regular visiting teacher at Willowbog Bonsai.

More information can be found on his very extensive website: www.bonsaiinformation.co.uk

chapter 1

The Bonsai Tradition

IN THE WEST WE USUALLY TEND TO THINK OF BONSAI AS A PURELY JAPANESE ART. BUT IT ORIGINATED IN CHINA AND KOREA OVER TWO THOUSAND YEARS AGO. IN CHINA, IT ALSO BECAME KNOWN AS *PENJING* OR *PENSAI* WHEN IT WON SUBSTANTIAL POPULARITY THERE A THOUSAND YEARS LATER.

Bonsai developed out of the Chinese love for the landscape of their mountains. They collected trees from mountaintops and grew them in their gardens to recreate the world that they so admired. Chinese opera, art, and culture draw from many sources, but some of the most influential are the mountains and deep, mysterious landscapes of Guilen in the south of China, which have been written about by scholars and painted by artists for centuries.

They created substantial landscapes in their wonderful gardens with peaceful ponds and miniature mountains created from limestone rocks taken from the lakes and rivers. It is interesting that from the making of gardens came the study of Chinese "scholars' stones" and Japanese "viewing stones," or *suiseki.* Prized by learned men for centuries, these stones were instantly popular in Japan and Korea and today command a huge following all over the world.

The stones were intended to resemble the mountains, landscapes, or objects and are nature's own works of art. In

△ Japanese woodblock print of Chrysanthemum bonsai, 19th century

△ Object stone: baboon, basalt, Scotland   △ Plateau stone, Italy   △ Hut stone, South Africa   △ Mountain stone, granite, Scotland

Japan, during the Meiji period in around 1650, a duke exchanged an entire castle for a particularly wonderful stone. Many *suiseki* were displayed beside a bonsai, because both objects were nature in miniature. Today, we display with or without bonsai and many bonsai enthusiasts also collect *suiseki* and enjoy going out to the mountains and beaches looking for landscape or object stones.

The Chinese kept the trees they collected from the mountains and displayed them in ceramic pots, lacquer trays, or on slabs of rock. They would also plant them on tall-fissured rocks, so that the image would emulate the tall limestone mountains of Guilen.

Although the art and craft of bonsai began over two thousand years ago, it developed slowly and different regions of China, Korea, and Japan created their own way of making these small trees special to their regional and artistic personalities.

Many ancient and great civilizations were interested in creating gardens. We may think one of the ancient Wonders of the World was the Hanging Gardens of Babylon, but the Chinese had wonderful gardens a thousand years before Babylon. The art of Chinese garden design is almost three and a half thousand years old and we know of detailed texts that still survive explaining the mathematical computations of planning a garden.

The lands occupied by desert nations were not always barren and many ancient stories of fields and gardens still abound in sacred texts, such as the Pharoanic texts of 3500 BCE that describe small trees placed in cut-out holes around tombs and palaces. The Arab nations were particularly fond of building gardens that inspired closeness to Allah. They were not allowed to make figurative images but could create great spaces and decoration with geometric and mathematical accuracy such as can still be found at Granada in Spain.

In China today, although many gardens were abandoned or destroyed during the Cultural Revolution, the people have either restored or rebuilt many of the famous gardens according to the original plans, which were recreations of nature in miniature.

△ Water is an intrinsic part of Chinese and Japanese garden design.
The Japanese garden, Brooklyn Botanic Gardens

△ The entrance to the Alhambra shows perfect lines and mathematical shapes to instill peace

Now, we come to the tree in a pot, or the *penjing*, which is the art of miniaturization that brings the majesty of huge landscapes or massive trees into our homes.

Used as art or decoration, *penjing* and *suiseki* were a means to assist meditation. *Penjing* was, and still is, popular as a hobby among religious groups, including Buddhists, and many temples have large collections of miniature trees. It was not just the miniaturized trees that brought joy, but the meditation derived from the discipline of creating these masterpieces. The art required dedication and commitment to learning, planning, and thought. As a bonsai grower, you will quickly find that pruning and caring for your tree will remove the stress of the outside world, as you focus completely on your bonsai. I am always amazed at how relaxed I feel after working with my trees.

It is interesting to consider the history of horticulture in China. The Chinese have been writing books on horticulture since CE 500. Many of these ancient texts discuss the reasons and techniques of air layering, seed propagation, and grafting.

In one of the gardens in the old capital of Xi'an (the city of the Terracotta Army), sits one of my own *penjing*, sent to the people of Xi'an by the City of Edinburgh as an exchange gift from one city to the other, twinned by culture and art.

The word bonsai derives from the Chinese word *pensai*. *Pensai* is a tray landscape of mixed trees and rocks and was first used as a general description of a miniature tree around 500 years ago, when the first of the small trees were exported from China to Japan. There are many styles now and I will look at these later.

chapter 2

Getting Started

THE WORD BONSAI COMES FROM THE JAPANESE, "BON" MEANING TRAY AND "SAI" MEANING PLANTING. THE GROWING OF BONSAI OR *PENJING* HAS BEEN ACCEPTED AS AN ART IN BOTH JAPAN AND CHINA FOR HUNDREDS OF YEARS.

What is a bonsai?

A bonsai or indeed a *penjing* must be clearly representative of a tree in miniature. In *penjing*, while that also applies, a wider range of symbolism is represented in the 30 or so styles that have been accepted for some 1,000 years. These styles can represent animals or, in the case of Singaporean bonsai, signs for health and good luck. However, Chinese, Korean, and Singaporean bonsai follow a more naturalistic style and are generally a little less regimented than Japanese bonsai.

It is precisely this fact that has led many countries to develop their own unique styles using the material found locally. Gary

△ *Juniper sabina*   △ European Black pine

△ Scots pine in *Bunjin* style

Marchal, from Louisiana, creates bonsai from Bald cypress, known also as Swamp cypress (*Taxodium distichum*), following the tree's natural inclination to develop a flat top as it grows very old. Obviously Gary will not live for two hundred or three hundred years but he is able, through his art, to make a tree that looks like an ancient Swamp cypress—one that looks as though it had been in the depths of the Louisiana swamps for over a century, but in fact has been created within only four to five years.

Salvatore Liporace will do the same with the material he has available in Italy, such as the ancient junipers he collects from the high mountains. Miniaturized into strange shapes by the elements, he starts working on these lost trees and within three or four years can create a masterpiece. I do the same with pines and yew collected from the Welsh or Scottish mountains.

We all have our techniques that allow us to grow and develop bonsai using native material.

Growers in all countries will create representations of the trees they see in their respective landscapes. Essentially a bonsai should look like a full-size tree in nature. The techniques I will show you can allow you to do this easily.

△ A normal-sized Black pine...   △ ...and this is the illusion of bonsai

Who keeps bonsai?

Anyone can keep a bonsai. However, if you're an artistic person who likes nature, enjoys the mountains and the landscapes, and is awed by, and feels especially close to trees, then keeping bonsai should suit you well.

In today's world it is now not only a hobby and an art form, but also part of design, both indoors and outdoors. Few modern homes are without an attractive example somewhere. Nor do you have to be rich to afford onei: they can be very inexpensive to buy from nurseries. Huge amounts of specially grown bonsai are created for the Western market. Ranging in price in price from a few dollars to many hundreds, they offer a wide choice and variety for the newcomer.

One or two questions often pose themselves for someone contemplating the purchase of bonsai. The first is that of time and involvement. As with everything that is alive, there is some work to do to ensure that your lovely bonsai tree stays healthy. This involves watering, feeding, pruning, occasional transplanting, and a good source of light. The bonsai does not appreciate extremes of heat or cold. In fact keeping a bonsai is just like looking after a houseplant. I can hear the wails of the person who says, "Oh, no—I can't keep any plants alive!" Why not? It is probably neglect that kills a plant. Sometimes overwatering can also be detrimental to the plant's health but, really, it is not an issue as long as you follow the care directions given later..

1 A selection of bonsai in a nursery
2 A good bonsai nursery will have a wide choice of pots for your trees

3 Natural bonsai material like this in Zion National Park in Utah is best left alone as it is a very famous tree in this region.
4 Superb collected Larch, styled by Liporace, Italy

Your first steps with bonsai

Let us assume you have bought your first bonsai (and we'll be looking at ways of acquiring bonsai shortly). What should you do then? Joining a club is a very good idea, since that will allow you to learn from other enthusiasts. The next thing is to find out what kind of bonsai you have. Does it grow indoors or outdoors? I always advise that the way to find out more about bonsai (apart from reading this book!) is to speak to a local bonsai nursery, who will be happy to give advice and may even organize workshops and classes. Some nurseries also have their own bonsai clubs to help their regulars as well as beginners. At a good bonsai nursery, you can see bonsai in all styles and all varieties. Never buy an expensive plant until you have learned the basics of looking after a single tree. Growing bonsai is not dissimilar from growing houseplants, so it will not take long to learn these basics.

Local garden centers will have a good selection of hardy shrubs for making into bonsai. You need a fast-growing tree since you need speed to design a bonsai. Otherwise, you will be waiting for years before anything moves.

Look for a plant with low-growing branches, because that will indicate a good surface-root spread. This is the most desirable feature in a bonsai, followed by good taper (or how the tree grows to a nicely shaped top or apex).

If collecting trees from the wild you must follow basic rules. While much land is public land, it is wise to check with local ordinance planning for the perimeter of national parks and forestry, and you may need to ask permission from farmers or other local groups.

Be clear about what you can take and what you cannot look after. Get to know the requirements of the species you are lifting. Lift only at the right time of the season, because the tree will die if you take it at the wrong time. Finally, joining a club can be a big help, since it means you have experienced growers to guide you.

Indoor and outdoor bonsai

Indoor bonsai

Most people start growing bonsai because they've been given one as a gift or have seen one at an exhibition or nursery. What is rarely clear to people is that there are basic horticultural requirements that have to be addressed. The vast majority of beginners automatically think that bonsai are kept inside a house and will make a nice decoration on a shelf or on the top of a television. It depends on the climatic conditions of your country. Many city dwellers want to grow bonsai but make the mistake of buying unsuitable species to grow inside an air-conditioned or centrally heated house or apartment.

If you live in a city in temperate climates such as northern Europe or northern parts of the USA or Canada, you will be able to grow warmth-loving species indoors, such as figs, serrisa or fukien tea bonsai, but not ones like pines and junipers, which prefer outdoor conditions, outdoors. If, on the other hand, you live in the southern USA or southern Europe, you can grow almost anything outdoors except in the cold of winter.

You would find it difficult to grow northern species indoors or in some cases even outdoors, because, again, species from colder climates do not easily adapt to warmer regions. Air conditioning, while cooling the air, is very drying and so not suitable for trees from colder climes.

Outdoor bonsai

Most bonsai are kept outdoors. You can keep bonsai on verandas, in gardens and even in a window box. The depth and range of available plants for outdoor collections is vast and the variety of species and size is astonishing—from tiny bonsai a few inches high to massive bonsai that are over several feet tall and need two or three people to lift them. From a shrub to the giant redwood, almost every tree can be made into a bonsai.

Outdoor bonsai need fresh air and a veranda or porch that is protected from winds and has some shade is a good place to keep a bonsai or two. Many people prefer outdoor bonsai because they can plan an oriental garden around their collection—but be wary of building up too big a one. Having too many trees may mean you end up struggling to look after a burgeoning variety of bonsai of different sizes and with varying care and maintenance needs..

1 Norway spruce group. 37" x 54" (94 x 137 cm).

2 Landscape using unusual stones and Miniature honeysuckle created by Koos le Roux, South Africa. 30" x 30" (75 x 75 cm)

3 Specimen of White Pine 48" (120 cm) tall and 100 years old

4 Slender Chinese juniper 38" (95 cm) tall and 12 years old.

Basic care

Let's look at the basic care regime for beautiful bonsai before we move on—here is a three-point checklist that looks at indoor and outdoor specimens. Care as a whole will be looked again in more detail in the following chapter.

1. Position

Deciduous indoor trees—leafed trees that lose their leaves in the winter until spring—should be kept in a cool room. Check the soil and keep it slightly damp, which may mean watering once a week in most cases. Just keep checking the soil and watch for dryness. Also, watch for tiny buds developing on the twigs, since that indicates that the tree is ready to burst back into life. In some cases, I have seen a bonsai lose all its leaves over the course of a week, then sit for a week, and then start to grow again. Species that come under this heading include elm and zelkova.

- Do not keep them in a perpetually shaded or sunny area, and make sure that you have easy access to watering.
- Do not keep in an elevated position where a bonsai can be lifted by the wind.
- Be sensible about displaying your bonsai in a position that can be seen by other people outside your garden. They could just get stolen!

2. Feeding

Feed once a week through the growing season, that is, spring through fall. Feed at half strength with a normal houseplant food such as Miracle Grow or Baby Bio. Increase to full strength in the late spring and reduce in midsummer to half again, and then use a low-nitrogen plant food, such as a tomato fertilizer, in the late summer to mid-fall.

Do not feed unless the tree is actually growing. Indoor trees will slow their growth in winter if you allow the tree to become a little cool. If the bonsai is kept at a regular temperature all year round, it will continue to grow. It is still better to reduce feeding to give the roots a rest over winter. Spray with a little liquid fertilizer each week, too. This is called foliar feeding.

3. Pruning and shaping

All that food will cause the tree to grow and become very healthy, and it will become bushier. You will now need to keep the tree in shape by trimming and pruning. It is really easy. Get a sharp pair of bonsai scissors designed not to tear the twigs. Hairdressing scissors can be used, because they, like bonsai scissors or shears, do not have a flat edge on one side, but two sharp edges.

On most shapes you simply cut back to the first set of new leaves at the top of the tree, then the second set round the middle of the tree, and the third set of leaves at the bottom. What I mean about set of leaves is that you count the leaves back from where they start to grow to the tip and count up one, two, or three sets of leaves—or pairs of leaves—and cut off the rest.

◁ Throughout the growing period, trim overlong
shoots to develop the shape of your bonsai

◁ 1st set at top

◁ 2nd set at mid area

◁ 3rd set at bottom

Buying bonsai

Most bonsai can be bought from specialist bonsai nurseries, and that is really the place to start. They will give you a choice, good advice, selection of species, accessories, and books.

Supermarkets and do-it-yourself stores may also sell bonsai but the staff do not generally know anything about them, so you may be buying a tree that is somewhat lacking in life. Day markets, garage sales, and the like are not the best place to buy. Stick to the specialist bonsai centers. But, no matter where you buy a bonsai, just ask yourself one question: Does this bonsai look like a miniature tree? If not, then it's not a bonsai.

Too many times have I seen garden shrubs for a few dollars placed in a ceramic pot and sold for 20 or 30 times the price of doing that yourself. They look like garden shrubs but with the magic label "bonsai." The buyer needs to think about it carefully and look at the tree and not the attractive pot and a few bits of rock.

Before you start, remember to ask some pertinent questions. Most bonsai nurseries I know are very well run and the owners and staff are very helpful. They should not object to your questions if they are a bona fide business.

Bonsai nurseries offer good advice, many run regular courses and generally ensure that you have the knowledge to grow, style or create a bonsai. There are many nurseries who dedicate themselves to bonsai because their owners are real enthusiasts. Every city has one or two specialists and you can find these in local telephone Yellow Pages or on the internet. There are also links on my own web site at www.bonsaiinformation.co.uk you can try out.

△ Developing maples' strength at the apex allows the leader bud to grow strongly before trimming

Here are some useful questions to ask a specialist.

Do you guarantee the tree will live if I follow your directions exactly?

Get a reasonable time frame here. A tree should last for at least six months and after that, with correct care, for as long as you own it.

Is it recently imported or grown on site?

If recently imported, make sure that the soil has been changed. Some imported trees can come potted in pure clay. As that is not a good growing medium, it should be discarded..

Important tips when buying a bonsai

When you buy a bonsai check carefully that all the branches are full of life. A shriveled bark and poor coloration of the foliage indicate dessication. You should examine it carefully before you take it away, but sometimes you may not notice problems until you get your plant home. You now need to return the bonsai as soon as you can. If the tree is dead then you may well have bought an already dead tree.

Good bonsai nurseries do not purposefully sell dead or dying bonsai but you have certain legal rights that should ensure that you receive a product that is fit for its intended purpose. If you bought a tree that was supposed to be alive and followed the instructions carefully—as given in writing by the seller—and, after a couple of weeks, or even months, the tree dies, then do not assume it was your fault. The responsible nursery will wish to exchange the tree.

Is this an indoor or outdoor bonsai? What is its name?

With this knowledge, you can refer to this book for tips on care.

How long is it since the tree was repotted?

The answer to this question tells you whether the tree has good soil and whether, therefore, it will survive for at least two years before it needs repotting.

You could also ask if the nursery can give you a written care sheet for your chosen species.

Starter, semitrained, and completed bonsai

When you buy a bonsai, it is in one of three conditions: starter, semitrained, or completed.

STARTERS are grown as bonsai material. They can be anything from one-year-old seedlings to large collected trees grown on in boxes for the experienced bonsai artist. The key point is that they have not been trained and will need wiring, feeding to develop growth, and pruning and shaping.

Some are used in bonsai workshops and are an excellent way to learn techniques. Avoid leggy material and take only the material that has lots of growth, since it is easier to make a bonsai out of something rather than nothing.

SEMITRAINED is material that has had some training, but check for how long. This will be the bonsai you will see on most benches in nurseries, because most of the stock is material for you to develop.

Is the tree healthy-looking, and showing no dried twigs or leaves? Look out for the wire biting into the trunk or branches because it is very hard to grow that out. If the soil is rising above the pot, the tree has not been repotted for a long time.

COMPLETED is something of a misnomer, because bonsai are growing and developing all the time. A completed tree is one where the design is completed at that stage in the tree's development. The bonsai does not, however, stop growing. Many nurseries sell completed trees in all sizes and species. Some are a few years old, are nicely shaped, and are, to all intents and purposes, completed, while others are "specimen" bonsai and are very expensive and reflect many years of work.

If you are buying a specimen bonsai do make sure that you get as much information about its care as you can.

▽ Young seedling trees being trained for bonsai

△ Semitrained material   △ A completed bonsai

◁ Wild *Taxodium* in the swamps of Louisiana

Collecting trees from the wild

Many serious bonsai enthusiasts and artists collect from the wild, because they know what to do during the delicate operation, just when to lift, how much root to cut off, and the aftercare required once they have taken their precious plant home.

Some bonsai masters who collect

Gary Marchal

In Louisiana, Gary Marchal, a bonsai master, grows many varieties, but specializes in Bald cypress (*Taxodium distichum*) from the Louisiana swamps. This is a popular species around the entire humid southern states, since it adapts readily to bonsai culture and produces magnificent bases.

Buttonwood, or *Conocarpus erectus*, is an unusual semitropical species. It has the tendency to develop huge areas of dead wood, which is prized by bonsai artists. In bonsai art, these areas of *shari*, or dead trunk areas, simulate great age.

Buttonwoods need a lot of feeding and watering. They are very vigorous when made into a bonsai, can take regular pruning, and will quickly develop into great trees.

Mary Madison

Mary Madison, a popular bonsai master from Florida, also collects *Taxodium*, although she is better known for her buttonwood bonsai.

▽ Gary Marchal with some of his collected swamp cypresses ▽ Bald cypress (*Taxodium distichum*)

△ Mary Madison with one of her little buttonwoods

▽ A forest of common junipers

△ But a miniature forest

△ Natural cascade pine in Zion National Park, Utah

△ This is a natural juniper in Red Canyon, Utah and shows the elements that the bonsai collector looks for. Junipers are common in the northern hemisphere, but may not be collected from National Parks.

Planting bonsai

Taking cuttings

You are pruning your tree and you want to plant the twigs in a pot so that they grow. Most of the cuttings can be used for miniature bonsai, landscape planting, rock planting and many more planting styles that need a little bonsai a few inches high.

Here's what you do:

1 Take your cuttings in the spring. Pictured here are *Cryptomeria* cuttings. Use either hardwood (older parts such as twigs or branches) or softwood (new shoots)

2 Remove a little of the bark from the base of the cutting if taking a hardwood cutting, and foliage if taking a softwood cutting

3 Have your pots already prepared with seed or cutting compost that is very light and allows fast development of roots

4 Wet the ends of the cutting in water and dip into rooting hormone powder, preferably without a fungicide

5 Using a chopstick or pencil, make a hole in the soil.

6 Place the cutting into the soil to a depth just above the area with the hormone powder so it sits just under the soil and is not too deep. Press slightly around the cutting to secure. Keep in a warm place and mist with water twice a day to create humidity. Watch for botrytis, a fungus that may attack cuttings in a warm humid atmosphere. Ensure that the cutting also has good air circulation.

7 After six months the roots will have developed sufficiently to require repotting.

Growing from seed

Forget about those so-called bonsai seed kits, and go for the real thing. Just walk around in the summer and pick up plenty of little seedlings for free. Remember, though, that bonsai is extremely difficult to grow from seed, so, although possible, it is not necessarily the best method. It is much easier to buy an inexpensive starter tree and develop that instead. Growing from a cutting is a much faster and more certain way of achieving success.

Tools and equipment

There are tools for every art, and bonsai is no exception.

You will need:

- a pair of bonsai shears
- angle cutters
- wire cutters
- wire
- a small turntable

As you develop, you may decide to add Wen or knob cutters, branch benders, different scissors for different jobs, and wire holders to your tool collection. As you get even more involved, you could consider angle or die grinders for carving, hobby-craft or Dremel machines for fine carving, clamps, and other tools, though you will use these less often.

1 Wire cutters; whether or not you use copper or aluminum wire you should not cut wire with anything else. They come in two sizes. Jinning pliers are used to crush the bark slightly prior to removing it to create jinns, the term used to describe dead branches. They are flatter than normal pliers and less damaging. Also used to twist wire when tying into a pot.

2 Angle cutters are the most useful of all the tools as these are used to shorten and remove branches if required. Always use a sealing agent to cover cuts. An assortment of Wen (knob), half Wen and angle cutters. Wen are full round cutters used to make a shallow depression when removing a branch, half Wen are used to cut in more detail.

3 A close up of the cutting head of a Wen.

4 Shears come in all sizes but essentially you need to keep the edge sharp or you will tear the cut and that can cause damage to the tree. Cuts must be clean and sealed. Wide handled shears are used for root and general trimming. Narrow handled shears allow more delicate work. Long, narrow blade shears are spring loaded and allow cuts to be made in awkward areas as the blades are narrower and longer.

5 Brushes are available from most dealers and are used to clean debris from the surface of your pot after trimming.

6 Goggles must be worn when working with power tools. Also wear a dust mask. Some people prefer to wear latex or rubber gloves for plucking prickly junipers, also for repotting to avoid transferring possible problems from one tree to another.

7 Branch benders are used to slowly bend thicker branches. Always protect the branch with plastic or at the least raffia prior to doing this. Tweezers are for the removal of moss and insects.

8 Large angle cutters are used for heavy branches or roots. Branch or trunk splitters are really for more advanced work when we need to remove living material from dead wood in order to rearrange the shape or bend into a new position. The hook is used to remove old soil when repotting.

9 Power tools are used to remove wood quickly and, as you get more experienced at bonsai, you will find them increasingly useful. They are also used for making stands for bonsai or *suiseki*.

10 A number of bits are used in power tool carving. Brushes are used with drills while the cutters are used with routers or special electrical carving tools.

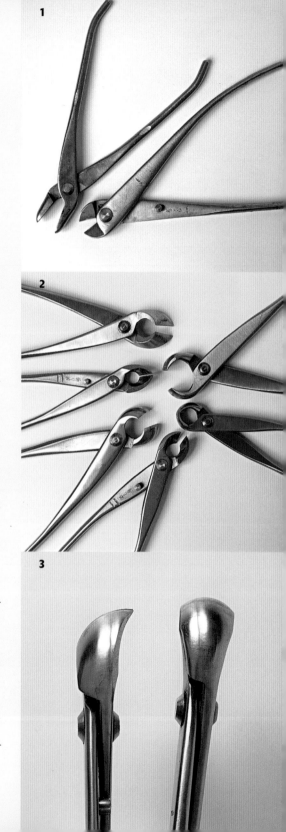

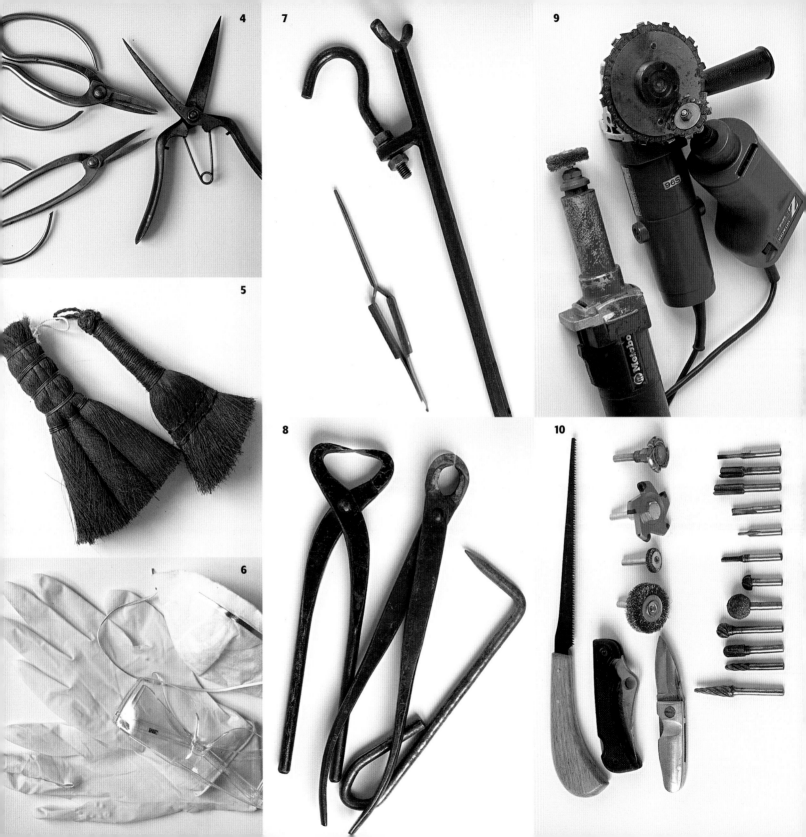

chapter 3

General Care

KEEPING YOUR BONSAI HEALTHY DEMANDS ONLY A LITTLE TIME AND EFFORT. APART FROM CORRECT PLACEMENT TO ENSURE ADEQUATE LIGHT AND THE RIGHT TEMPERATURE, THE MAIN THINGS YOU NEED TO KNOW ABOUT ARE HOW OFTEN AND WHEN TO WATER AND FEED YOUR BONSAI WITHOUT OVER- OR UNDERDOING EITHER.

△ These are small-sized bonsai grown from cuttings and less than 6" (15 cm) in height

FEEDING allows the bonsai to develop. What you want is a fast-growing bonsai so that successive trimming or pruning will in turn make it put out lots of growth that becomes dense and mature-looking to the viewer.

WATERING is important. It varies according to the time of year and the species, so consult the chart on pages 34-37 for directions.

POTTING will be done once every two or three years on a bonsai that is not fully completed or mature.

SHAPING your bonsai is an ongoing process but there are preferred times within the growing season to do this. (see the chart, pages 34-37)

DEFOLIATING is when you remove all the leaves in order to force a fresh crop. This is usually done in the early to midsummer. Cut off the leaves, just below the leaf itself, leaving a little stalk. That allows a slow die-back to the next bud at the base of the leaf stalk, which will quickly develop. Treat as for spring when the new leaves are growing. Most species can be repotted after defoliation. This technique helps the tree make more foliage and smaller leaves.

Protecting over the winter is essential in temperate and colder climates, and protecting your bonsai in hot climates is equally important through the hottest summer months.

▷ Informal azalea 36" (90 cm) tall and five years in training
▷ **INSET** Rowan with its berries in the fall

Care charts

These charts are for quick and easy reference. Please remember that this is purely a general guide. You will know your local temperature and, in the case of warmer or tropical areas, winter will not be an issue, but it's best to try to give the trees a rest. For example in the USA, Washington State can be temperate in places while Florida is subtropical and very humid (although I have experienced snowfall in northern Florida!). Northern Australia is much hotter than southern Australia. You know the local climate in your own area, so adjust to its requirements.

Location

Outdoor trees

Jobs to do	Watering	Feeding	Pruning or shaping	Potting or shaping	Protection or location
Early spring	Water once a week using tepid water. Don't water if soil is damp. Don't water if trees are not growing but keep soil a little damp.	Do not start feeding yet.	Shape conifers and deciduous trees as long as growth is not apparent.	This is a good time for potting conifers.	Keep trees slightly cool and start giving good light. Keep all trees protected against extremes of weather.
Mid-spring	As above but watch for growth, which may need a little more water. Watch for pests.	Do not feed until the buds are growing well.	Very light pruning but always seal cuts. Shape conifers.	If buds are growing it is too late, but this is also a good time for conifers. Deciduous species can be repotted.	As above, but conifers should be fine outside from early spring onward.
Late spring	Water three times a week if soil is getting dry.	Feed if buds are growing well.	Stop pruning if trees are in budding mode. If not, this will be the last period.	Deciduous species if buds are not growing.	As above, but deciduous trees may be fine outside now apart from maples in windy areas
Early summer	You may have to increase to once a day or even twice now.	Full-strength feed for young trees and half-strength for mature trees. Mature trees can also use pellet-form slow-release feed such as Bio Gold.	Leave trees to grow now and start watching pine candles (a word often used to mean buds). Prune if required.	Too late for spring repotting.	Take all bonsai out of winter protection to get them used to outside conditions in colder areas However protect flowering species from high winds.
Mid-summer	Increase to twice now. Spray mist the foliage. Watch for pests.	Do not feed because trees are now in a semidormant condition and are less likely to take up food. Warm and tropical areas are the only exception, but it is best to give trees a rest.	Defoliate if required the following species (there are more but local growers will advise): elms (*Ulmus*, *Zelkova*), hornbeam (*Carpinus*), apple (*Malus*), birch (*Betula*), maple (*Acer*), quince (*Chaenomeles*), olive (*Olea*) pomegranate (*Punica*), willow (*Salix*).	You can repot after defoliation. Bald cypress (*Taxodium*) can also be repotted in summer. Ideal time to reshape or design most deciduous species.	Shade in hot areas and partial shade elsewhere. Shade after repotting and avoid extremes of weather. Build a simple net shade house if you have a number of bonsai.

Jobs to do	Watering	Feeding	Pruning or shaping	Potting or shaping	Protection or location
Late summer	As above if still hot but if getting cold reduce to once a day. In hotter areas continue as before.	Start feed now with low-nitrogen 0-10-10 or tomato feed. Check your local brand names and descriptions. Trace elements should still be in feed. Biogold etc. are fine.	Wire and prune pines, junipers, yew (*Taxus*) etc. All deciduous species should be finished by now.	No potting now other than bald cypress, (*Taxodium*) buttonwood (*Conocarpus*) cotoneaster, fig (*Ficus*), most tropical trees. Investigate locally.	As above. Late summer sun is still hot.
Early fall	Once a day unless in a hot area.	Stop feed when deciduous leaves start to change color Continue feed at half strength on evergreens.	Wiring can be done on junipers, cryptomerias and Japanese cypress, Tropical trees can also be worked but it is getting late now.	Preferably no potting now, especially in cold and temperate regions, since the trees do not have much time to recover before winter sets in.	If high, hot sun is gone, remove shade. Spray mist the foliage and check for pests and soil pests.
Mid-fall	Once a day unless in a hot area.	No feed to deciduous but half-strength once a fortnight to evergreens.	Most species cannot take any work at this interim time.	No potting.	Whatever light is available. Continue to turn the pots once every few days.
Late fall	Three to four times a week unless leaves have fallen, then just keep slightly damp and not soggy. The tree is unable to take in water when there are no leaves.	No feed to deciduous but half-strength once a fortnight to evergreens.	Most species cannot take any work at this interim time.	No potting.	Whatever light is available. Continue to turn the pots once every few days.
Early winter	Keep soil damp. Water maybe three times a week.	No feed except pellet food on evergreens but remove before cold weather starts.	If maples (Acer) are naked now for at least a month, major pruning can be carried out at this time. However, it is better to wait until late winter, giving the trees a month before new growth starts. Seal all cuts.	No potting.	Put delicate trees into a shaded glasshouse or winter quarters. Deciduous bonsai do not need light after fall in cold climates but need to be cool.
Mid-winter	Just when the soil needs it. Evergreens are still slowly growing, so be sure to keep an eye on them. Keep out of wind if freeze sets in your region.	No feed at this time.	No work at this time.	No potting.	Protect all trees from bad weather. If stored in a glasshouse, fully shade glass and do not allow heat build up on sunny winter days.
Late winter	Just when the soil needs it. Evergreens are still slowly growing so be sure to keep an eye on them. Keep out of wind if freeze sets in your region.		If maples (Acer) are naked now for at least a month, major pruning can be carried out at this time, giving the trees a month before new growth starts. Seal all cuts.	No potting.	Protect all trees, especially in cold weather.

Indoor trees

Jobs to do	Watering	Feeding	Pruning or shaping	Potting or shaping	Protection or location
Early spring	Water once a week in normal room temperature by immersing the bonsai completely, if small enough, into a sink or clean washbowl.	Only if you see the leaves are growing.	Light nipping of overgrown branches.	This is the season to refresh the pot. Repot with fresh soil.	Light, bright conditions now. Avoid—in any month—burning sun coming through a window, and turn every other day for even light.
Mid-spring	If the tree needs it, water twice a week, once by immersion if a small tree, and once by watering normally.	Only if you see the leaves are growing. Once every two weeks at half strength.	Light nipping of overgrown branches.	This is the season to refresh the pot. Repot with fresh soil.	Light, bright conditions now. Avoid—in any month—burning sun coming through a window, and turn every other day for even light.
Early summer	The tree can be watered once a day if it needs it. If the soil is damp don't water. Mist every day. Do not immerse after this until next year.	Once a week, at full strength.	Prune out overlong branches that have grown in the spring. Always leave one or two sets of new leaves.	It's best if you do not repot now unless you understand the species' requirements.	If the weather is good, the indoor tree can be placed outside now. If you have a veranda or porch, beware of drafts and wind. While the tree likes outside air, slight protection is advisable. Turn every other day for even light.
Mid-summer	The tree can be watered once a day if it needs it. If the soil is damp don't water. Mist every day.	Do not feed.	Most design work can be done now: wiring, shaping and pruning, and defoliating techniques.	Repot if defoliating.	If the weather is good, the indoor tree can be placed outside now. If you have a veranda or porch, beware of drafts and wind. While the tree likes outside air, slight protection is advisable. Turn every other day for even light.
Early fall	The tree can be watered once a day if it needs it. If the soil is damp don't water. Mist every day.	Low-nitrogen feed, once a week at full strength.	No work.	No repotting.	Bring tree back in, because the weather changes. Otherwise, keep in a bright place and turn every other day for even light.

Jobs to do	Watering	Feeding	Pruning or shaping	Potting or shaping	Protection or location
Late fall	Keep damp and spray three or four times a week.	Low-nitrogen food once a week at half strength. Do not feed if leaves change color.	No work.	No repotting.	Keep in a bright place and turn every other day for even light. If leaves fall keep cool until early spring.
Early winter	Keep damp and spray three times a week.	If leaves are changing color, do not feed any more.	No work.	No repotting.	Keep in a bright place and turn every other day for even light.
Mid-winter	Keep damp and spray two or three times a week	Do not feed.	No work.	No repotting.	Keep in a bright place and turn every other day for even light.
Late winter	Keep damp and spray twice a week if kept in a warm area, or once a week if in a cool area, or not at all if in a cold area.	Do not feed.	No work.	Repot into early spring from now.	Keep in a bright place and turn every other day for even light.

◁ Mid-summer is the ideal time to work on most trees as it is a dormant period with another growth period happening shortly after. Check the best time for your area. A workshop guided by a teacher is a good way of learning.

Where you place your bonsai is very important. Get it right and it will survive, but get it wrong and it will join the long list of those specimens over which the usual lament is spoken: "I bought a bonsai but it's dead. What should I do now?" It's a question that newcomers around the festive holiday period often ask me! The charts on pages 34–37 will guide you, but let's look at a few points and some reasons why things go right or wrong.

Indoors

On a shelf is fine, but not above any electrical items. The bathroom is successful for many and bringing the bonsai in for display is fine as long as you do not bring it in from one extreme to the other during winter or colder months.

Windows are also a good place, but avoid closing a curtain on the bonsai. Putting it between the curtain and the cold window will harm the little tree as the curtains stop any heat getting to it—not that it needs a lot of heat, but it will have had a warm room temperature during the evening or day and then all that is suddenly taken away. This causes the leaves to fall off. The area around the bonsai will become cold and damp and problems could set in. The next day, you expose the poor little thing to heat all over again.

The simple trick is to keep an even temperature all the time. The bonsai will appreciate the temperature that you like. If it is kept in a cool humid area such as a bathroom or a spare room, then the tree will adapt. Most so-called indoor bonsai are simply normal trees from warmer areas or tropical and semitropical regions. Essentially, the care is the same as for a houseplant.

Turn your trees round every couple of days. This is very important because the light needs to get to all areas of your

△ Indoor bonsai are normally developed from trees originating in warm regions. They appreciate the even temperature.

bonsai and not just one side. This is where a turntable is useful if the bonsai is large.

After watering, tilt your bonsai for an hour or so. Get a little wedge of wood to stick under one side of the pot after watering to allow the soil to drain.

Summer is a good time to put your bonsai outside if it is sunny, because they will, like most houseplants, appreciate fresh air when it is warm. Just watch for pests, and spray if you need to. Bring them in when the weather starts to change but most indoor trees can stay out for up to three months in most temperate climates.

Among the many hundreds of species that can be grown inside, *Serrisa foetida*, *Sagerita theezans*, *Ehretia* (also known as

Carmona) *microphyla*, Chinese or Flowering privet, *Ligustrum sinense* are popular.

Outdoors

While people in the northern hemisphere call southern areas warm, those in the southern hemisphere call the northern areas warm. North Island in New Zealand is warm while South Island is cool, because it is nearer the South Pole. Northern Canada is cold while southern Canada is warmer. We divide the world by the Equator so my descriptions refer to the warmer areas closer to the center band of the earth.

The charts on pages 34–37 will guide you but here are the basic essentials.

Cold climates

Colder climates need bonsai protected through the colder months. Soft leaves that are developing, such as maple, can be easily damaged by winds in the early part of the year. Bring the deciduous trees out in late spring or early summer in cold climates.

In winter, you need to be aware that damp soil can become frozen and, if the foliage or upper portion of the bonsai is in any way exposed to wind, it can become freeze-dried. What happens is that the soil is frozen and the foliage is then whipped about by winds. As a result, it will soon dehydrate. This is the commonest cause of bonsai death over winter – not as a result of cold, but because the trees are exposed to wind.

In late spring or early summer, give the trees as much light as possible because the buds need all they can get. Place the trees in a sheltered area away from hard winds. Watch for late frosts in the early summer months.

Summer is when you need to be aware of burning sun. Slight shade is fine in exposed areas. However, usually, there is little problem in this climate. Remember to turn the trees around every few days. A good tip is to put a marker in the soil and make sure that all the markers are facing the same way from day one. Every few days, turn the trees round and, if the markers are all facing the same way, you know you're turning all your trees consistently.

Autumn usually means a late summer in colder areas, but watch for temperature changes and start putting the trees in after the leaves have changed, and even if there is a first frost. A first, light, frost forces fall in most deciduous bonsai.

Mid to temperate climates

Winter is when you need to protect bonsai from cold winds and snowfall until warmer weather starts, However, most coniferous species can be kept outside through the colder months.

Remember to turn the trees, however, because sunny days through the winter months will mean the foliage will grow toward the light. Use the marker method outlined under Cold climates above.

Most trees can be outside in spring. However, you should be careful with trees with softer leaves, such as maple. These need to harden their leaves off before you expose them to wind, rain, and sun.

Summer months mean that you will need to protect the trees from excessive sun. Put most species under a shade net if you live in the hotter areas of your country.

Autumn is as for spring.

Warm and hotter areas

In most cases, these areas will not experience colder weather, but it can happen occasionally. Keep an eye out over problematic months and bring more delicate trees into a covered area.

If you live in a country with a rainy season, you need to stop too much water getting into the pot. Do this by elevating one side through that period to allow the water to drain. Remember to change the tilt to allow even run-off. In general, always protect the bonsai from excessive weather conditions.

Summer months can be very hot and bright, so make sure the bonsai are shaded from excessive sun.

△ Shade netting is essential to protect bonsai from direct sun

△ A Giant Sequoia grown by Bill Sullivan. It is now housed in the Golden State Bonsai Federation (GSBF) North Collection in San Francisco

Quick tips on watering

- The soil should be free-draining, and that means when you water it the water flows freely through the soil without collecting on the surface.
- Keep the soil moist in the summer and winter, but water less in winter.
- Usually once a day in summer is enough but check your soil. If it is looking a little light in color, it is probably dry.
- In winter, outdoor bonsai will need a weekly check but, if damp, leave them.
- For indoor bonsai, watering once every two or three days is normal, but if your heating is running high then the soil will dry out faster. Keep the soil slightly damp but not soggy. A bonsai is like a houseplant in this respect.
- Cacti and succulents need little water during the three months of colder weather in temperate or colder climates, You should bear this in mind if you keep crassula or money-jade tree bonsai. They are succulents and should be watered once a month in winter or colder months.
- Spraying or misting with a fine spray once a day will be appreciated by your bonsai in the non-winter months. If you use a hothouse in the winter, then a weekly spray is acceptable.
- Spring watering in colder climates will be when and if the bonsai require it. In colder climates over the winter, outdoor bonsai need little if any water—assuming they remain outside, of course.

Watering

Although we have covered the general rules for watering in the care charts on pages 34-37., I will go into this in more depth, because it is very important. Lack of attention to proper watering can be the killer of bonsai. So read the "Quick tips" box here and follow the advice.

Watering systems

Automatic watering systems are fine as long as you watch that all the bonsai are getting their fair share. Use an automatic time switch, often called a computer watering system. What is not good about automatic systems, though, is that they can water when the tree does not need water; the drip feeds can clog or stop working; and the system, while partially controllable, will still

△ Some trees needs watering twice or three times a day in the summer

△ Swamp cypress may need a constant drip feed if the climate is warm, although they easily live outside their natural swamp conditions

water when there is rain. The systems I like have a "cloudy day" feature, but it can be very warm on a cloudy day and the soil will still need water. You can turn that feature off and the tree will be watered whether it needs water or not. That is not a bad thing some of the time, because the soil should be free-draining and the water, of course, will run through fast anyway. You can use wedges to tilt those bonsai that need less water and will benefit from free run-off, such as conifers. Alternatively, remove the drips from the pots every other day.

Hoses

Hose spraying is the usual method of watering. It can be a more controlled way of making sure the right trees get what they need. Use an adjustable trigger spray to control the intensity of the water delivery. Feeder units can also be added easily. Do not wash the soil away with too strong a jet.

Requirements for winter and summer watering depend on climate demands. You can check these out in the care chart on pages 34–37.

Misting

This means giving the foliage a fine spray, because that part of the bonsai also needs to have humidity levels kept up. Especially important in warmer climates, in hot weather, and under shade netting, this may need to be done twice a day. In colder climates, misting is rarely done in winter. In fact, in colder climates, the soil is kept just barely damp through the winter months. Because many trees need little light and water, there is a tendency to forget all about them. Remind yourself to check them out at least once a week as root rot or conversely root dryness can set in.

△ When watering a newly potted tree, use a fine mister or spray to avoid disturbing the roots

Light and air

INDOOR BONSAI need light but not a window that is facing the sun all day. That will fry the tree. Keeping your bonsai on a shelf is also acceptable as long as the shelf gets a lot of light during the day. It is very important to turn your trees regularly.

Do not put your bonsai in a window where you draw the curtains at night, because that will create a damp, cold place and chill the bonsai. Good even temperature is the answer. If it suits you, it will suit your bonsai. It is also not a good idea to keep bonsai on top of televisions and hi-fi units because any dripping water may create an electrical fire hazard.

OUTDOOR BONSAI need plenty of free air circulation. They need some sun but also some shade if the sun is hot. Do not place tight up against a wall or a fence, which prevents free circulation of air.

Turn your trees every few days to ensure even light. At least a half-turn every week so that over the month you get even growth. Otherwise, the tree will die on the side away from the light while the side facing the light will become very untidy. This, of course, applies to all houseplants.

Light in winter in cold climates is not so important, but fresh air is. In fact, all bonsai need a free flow of air around the foliage. This stops stifling air conditions and reduces the possibility of fungal infections on the leaves, roots, and soil. Botrytis is the most common of these and usually appears in damp, cool conditions. While it can be treated with a copper fungicide, it is better to prevent it in the first place.

It is important to make sure that you get good light or as much light as possible in the growing seasons. Trees in pots rarely appreciate full sun, because it dries out the shallow soil. The leaves, with no respite from the heat, will shrivel. Provide some shade for the crucial part of the day. That is fairly easy to check if you watch your garden during a sunny day and observe when the full sun hits your bonsai area.

Soil

All bonsai soil needs to be free-draining. The soil must not:

- hold too much water
- collect water on the surface
- remain soaked long after watering

To this end, most bonsai soils are created to drain rapidly. Single soils such as Akadama (general), Kureyu (conifers), and Kanuma (azaleas and acid lovers) are now available and your local bonsai specialist will help you with that. What you will use will depend on your species' requirement.

Here are some basics:

- Grit: Of the two types − rough and smooth − the former is preferable. Wash well to remove dust.
- Sand: Another name for grit. Not like sand on the beach, since that is far too fine for bonsai
- Organic: Rotted pine bark, leaf mold, peat moss, soilless compost.
- Loam: Comprises a mixture of the above, clay, and proprietary brands. It does not mean garden soil.
- Akadama: A general-purpose, brand-name soil of clay granules in differing sizes and qualities. For most deciduous species.
- Kanuma: As above but for acid-loving plants such as azaleas and satsukis..
- Kureyu: Conifer soil.

Preparation of soil

Single-material soils can also be mixed with organic material, because the former are sterile. Japanese and clay-type granular soils are designed to be water-retentive but allow free passage of excess water, and so will dry out quickly. If this is a concern in your area, mix with organic material. All trees planted in Japanese and single soils need feeding.

Pines require a soil with a higher grit or sand content. A normal blend is 70 percent grit to 30 percent organic. Some imported Japanese branded soils are used, but because they retain water, you must be extra careful about the watering requirements. Conversely, some imported soils are used on their own and sometimes mixed. In this case, the Akadama, Kanuma,

or whatever replaces the organic. Your local club, dealer, or expert will guide you.

For deciduous trees, the rule of thumb is around a 50:50 percent grit and organic, while, for tropical trees, a 70 percent organic base is used, with some grit for drainage through the soil. Some tropical bonsai can take higher clay content, but there are so many varieties that it is best you take local advice.

▽ Always sieve the fines out of soils as the dust will compact and cause drainage problems in your bonsai pot

△ The soils can be used neat, but many of these soils benefit from being mixed with other mediums such as grit and even other Japanese soils. However, only you or your teacher will understand the local requirements of the soils needed for your particular area

Potting and Repotting

Finding the right pot for the tree

Here a yew is planted in an oversize pot, making it look out of balance. The tree looks too small.

1 The tree in its training pot

2 The tree was removed from the existing pot, with care being taken not to disturb the roots too much during this operation. It was done in early spring—the right time for potting

3 One choice was a narrower but deeper pot. The pot looks too heavy and the tree is not balanced visually, so we reject this pot

4 We tried the tree in this shallower pot and felt that it looked a lot better

5 Preparing the pot is in the repotting section but here you see the pot with retaining wires in place. You can use string or plastic ties but I prefer 2 or 3 mm aluminum wire and not copper (it can act as a fungicide) wire to retain trees

6 We removed the soil where needed, trimmed the roots which were healthy, and mounded the tree up so that we could emulate a small hill. We also exposed the *nebari* or surface root structure. The stones were left in the roots as they were found with the tree originally and the tree had simply grown around them. They are limestone and seem to benefit the health of the tree, as it was growing on a limestone mountain originally. We carefully secured the tree with the wires using plastic or rubber tubing to protect the roots

7 Placing moss helps retain the soil when the tree is settling down

8 The finished bonsai in its new pot

Repotting

Your tree will fill the pot with roots and use up all the soil. Therefore, every two to four years you need to remove some of the roots and repot the tree so that it gets fresh soil. Young trees need repotting every two years while old, mature bonsai may not need repotting for four years, because they are established and slower-growing.

1 This *Zelkova* has been in its pot for four years, a year longer than it needed. The tree is suffering as its roots push it out of the pot. The edges of the roots are cut from inside to loosen the tree.

2 Remove the bonsai retaining wires.

3 Remove the tree.

4 Using a root hook, carefully remove the soil and untangle the roots without damaging the fine roots. Pay attention to the roots through the root mass, as well as checking for any insect attack, such as root aphids.

5 Now remove the soil near the trunk. Be careful during this part so as to avoid damage to the *nebari* (surface root structure).

6 Remove excess roots, normally about one third, but in this case half. Check for dead or rotten roots and seal and repair these at the same time. Seal all big root cuts with Kiyonal or Lac Balsam, otherwise you will get root rot.

7 Remove excess roots near the trunk that stop the free development of surrounding roots, which are important for branch development.

8 Carefully clean the main surface roots, the *nebari*, as these are exposed. During this procedure spray and mist the root structure every ten minutes to prevent the root mass drying out.

9 Cut the mesh to cover the holes in the pot to prevent the soil falling through.

10 Make mesh retainers to fix the mesh to the pot. Bend the wires into figure-six shapes.

11 Bend the tail of the figure-six on both sides, over the wire, and insert into the mesh.

12 The mesh sections have been placed on top of each hole and the wire retainer has been pushed through and bent on the underside of the pot. The long wires are retaining wires to secure the tree into the pot after repotting. This ensures the tree will not move when it is establishing new roots.

13 Sift out your soil from dust and discard the dust.

14 Mix the soils as required.

15 Mound the soil in the area you wish the tree to sit, center or off center. This mounding will force the dry soil into the base of the tree roots.

16 Gently work the tree into the mound. Add more soil and work in with your fingers. Sleeve the retaining wires with plastic or rubber tubing.

17 Finish off the surface and keep the *nebari* (surface roots) clear.

18 The finished *Zelkova serrata*. Water the new soil in thoroughly and leave for a week or until the soil dries out slightly. The tree cannot develop roots at this point, so avoid over-watering and do not feed for at least six weeks or you will burn the young developing roots.

Feeding

Your bonsai needs to be fed. It cannot live on water alone. Feeding is easy and, although you have the guide charts on pages 34-37, here is a breakdown of feeds and the basic regime.

- High nitrogen makes the leaves grow.
- Low nitrogen makes the branches, roots, and cambium (the under-bark) grow. Tomato fertilizer is low in nitrogen.
- 0-10-10 or similar is a zero nitrogen. Used with most pines at the beginning of the season and through the early stages of bud (or "candle") development. Also used with soft-leaved trees such as maples in the early flush of growth, because that helps the leaves become stronger. Used in the later part of the year just prior to fall or into the winter season in colder climes.
- For acid-loving plants use Miracid, or similar. Preferred by azaleas, for example.

Quick tips on feeding

SPRING: Half-strength when the buds are open—0-10-10. Build to full strength in late spring and use a high-nitrogen feed after the first flush of growth. Feed at half strength through most of the growing season in hotter areas.

SUMMER: If a hot area, do not fertilize. If a cool area, stop in midsummer. The trees can not absorb fertilizer at this time as they go into semidormancy because of the heat and stop growing.

AUTUMN: Reduce to half strength and use a low-nitrogen fertilizer, because that helps the bonsai into the main dormant season in cooler climes.

Proprietary plant food

Brand names differ throughout the world but generally it is fine to use any popular houseplant food, but not lawn or grass food, because they are far too high in nitrogen and can easily damage the roots. Here are some examples of useful products.

- General: Miracle Grow, Baby Bio, Peters.
- Specific to certain trees: in different forms—Chempack.
- Surface cakes to lie on the soil (and therefore slow-release): Green King, Bio Gold, rapeseed cake surface dressing.
- Low-nitrogen: 0-10-10, tomato fertilizer.
- Special: Miracid (for acid lovers).

Pests and Diseases

No matter where you are in the world, there are insect attack squadrons just ready to get at your beloved bonsai. Whether indoors or outdoors, there is something that fancies taking a nibble.

Indoor bonsai suffer from blackfly, mites, and whitefly. Occasionally they also receive careful attention from swarms of greenfly when they are outside.

You have to be prepared and fight the little critters off. Try these:

- Systemic insecticides. These go in through the roots and come out through the entire bonsai: bark, branches, and leaves. Slow-acting but successful.
- Foliar insecticides. Spray these chemicals onto the leaves and needles. Very quick-acting. Wear a face mask when spraying.
- Trunk and branch washes. Winter sprays that get at overwintering pests.
- Fungicides. Used in a powder form and mixed with water. It is safer using the powder than the liquid form. Protect the soil of pines when using.
- Cocktail. A mix of feed and insecticide to avoid the need to spray twice. Wear a face mask.
- Specific. Insecticides for specific problems such as vine weevil.

A little information about the enemy

1 Vine weevil larvae. Usually most visible at repotting time.

2 Vine weevil pupae.

3 Adult vine weevil. These can fly and lay thousands of eggs as soon as they hatch from the pupae.

4 Vine weevil leaf damage

5 Pine shoot moth pupae. The caterpillars eat the new shoots on pines and are prevalent in pine forests.

6 The pupae of the pine shoot moth

7 Sawfly larvae and skins with the results of a good day's chomping.

8 Willow aphid. They cause canker and subsequent die-back.

9 Blackfly adult and wingless nymphs. The winged females hunt in swarms

10 These are the winged blackfly adults.

11 Sooty mold is the fungus that is the residue of an aphid or adelgid attack. Wash off or, if really bad, spray with a copper fungicide

12 If you see a pine and it has bunches of cotton balls on the base of the needles, then most probably adelgids are present

13 Adelgids on a garden plant—beware: your bonsai may be next!

14 Greenfly, the most common of the aphids. Use systemic insecticide

15 Leaf damage of greenfly. The sap has been sucked and the leaf shriveled.

16 A greenfly, looked at in this light with the fine delicate tracery refracting rainbows, is a veritable jewel of an insect.

Pest problems and solutions

▽ Pine rust growing on the needles already affected by the residue of an aphid attack, which left sooty mold

Problem	Cause	Insecticide	Treatment	Other information
Sticky leaves.	Aphids. Greenfly are the most common. Blackfly can land in the evening and devastate a tree within 48 hours. They hide under the leaves, too, and are like black dots with legs.	Systemic and foliar. Aphids can be removed by hand but treat for further attacks.	Read pack. Foliar: Once every 7 days under and on top of the leaves. Systemic: In soil every 2 weeks.	A new systemic currently available is Provado, it is excellent for soft-leaved trees such as maples. You can also treat with lime sulfur: 2–4 drops per pint (half-liter).
Sticky leaves and small white insects under leaves.	Whitefly.	Systemic and foliar.	Read pack. Foliar: Once every 7 days under and on top of the leaves. Systemic: In soil every 2 weeks.	Wash off all traces with a spray or a hose. Treat under the leaves, too.
White cotton ball webs in pine-needle clusters. Sometimes other conifers.	Adelgids.	Systemic and foliar.	Read pack. Foliar: Once every 7 days under and on top of the leaves. Systemic: In soil every 2 weeks	Wash off all traces with a spray or a hose. Treat under the leaves, too. You can also treat with lime sulfur: 2–4 drops per pint (half-liter).
Lack of vigor, leaves not growing properly.	Vine weevil. Becoming a real problem in many countries.	There are specific treatments for this including Siskin Green and now Provado.	Check soil for grubs at repotting time. Read pack. Systemic: In soil according to instructions	A new systemic currently available is Provado. Used against vine weevil, it is excellent for soft-leaved trees such as maples.
Yellow stripes on pine needles.	Pine-needle cast (Lophodermium pinastre). This is a fungal disease.	Copper sulfur.	Read pack. Foliar: Once every 7 days under and on top of the leaves. Repeat every 7 days for at least 3 weeks to stop the fungal growth cycle.	It is important that the copper does not enter the soil level, as it will damage the beneficial mycelium in the roots. Protect with a cloth and plastic bag or sheeting over the soil.

△ Fungus - the multicellular body is mycelium.

Problem	Cause	Insecticide	Treatment	Other information
After winter damage on pines, weak growth on all trees.	Cold drafts, shaded too much, lack of watering. Lack of vigor in leaves can also mean the tree is not getting enough trace elements.		Top dressing with amino and nucleic acids, trace elements, and organic nutrients.	Top Dressing GK365 is a new product from Japan and many masters are impressed by it.
Thin growth, no vigor.	Insect attack in soil. Root aphid, leather jackets, etc.	Soil insecticide, systemic insecticide. Root-drench thoroughly.	Read pack. Once every 7 days.	Be careful you do not treat trees that do not take to a root-drench. Read pack.
Gray areas on leaves, small wet webs between leaves.	Botrytis/mildew. This is a fungal mold caused by turgid air and damp conditions. Affects anything but especially cuttings and young seedlings.	Fungicide, but be careful not to get it into soil.	There are brand-named treatments for botrytis or mildew so check with your bonsai nursery.	If this is happening change your air flow and get fresh moving air to your bonsai.
Gray-looking foliage on junipers and needle junipers.	Red spider mite. To check if this is in residence, put your hand under a branch and shake the branch. Tiny mites will drop onto your hand.	Systemic every 7 days until clear. Usually 5 weeks.	Read instructions.	A more common cause for concern than people realize. If you get Red Spider Mite then check all your needle foliage trees. If it is on one it's probably on the lot.
Holes in leaves.	Caterpillar attack, leaf-cutting bees, insects that like to chomp leaves!	First, check the underside of foliage and look for insects hiding. Look around the root area as well. Lift moss. Immediate foliar spray, followed by systemic.	Read instructions.	It is precisely why you need to spend at least 15 minutes a day checking your bonsai to reduce insect attack.
Weak growth with brown or gray lumps on the branches and trunk.	Sapsuckers, scale insects.	These require a little more work. Dip a cotton swab top in a little rubbing alcohol and rub off each one. Followed by a systemic soil drench and foliar spray.	Read instructions.	Check every spring and midsummer and especially before any winter dormancy.

Remember to remove some of the moss on the surface of your soil in the winter. It can harbor pests. Plant in a separate tray and treat with a systemic insecticide. It will be need to be reapplied in spring. Protect from birds by placing plastic mesh over the moss. Otherwise collect or cultivate fresh moss, but check for insects first before applying.

△ The wood-eating beetle,
Anoplophora formosiana

Base Rot

This Red pine, *Pinus densiflora*, was created using two side branches from a garden shrub. It has lost some area at the base because of rot and subsequent red spot fungal attack. This can happen if you keep a pine bonsai in too humid an area or do not allow the soil to dry out slightly between watering. Pines need to have that drying-out period and in the winter, spring, and late fall they need less water than deciduous trees. The problem is that many people tend to water all their bonsai at once, instead of working out individual needs. It is easy to sort this out by keeping species that need special attention in specific groups.This one acquired the rot because it had moss on the surface. This meant the base of the tree got too wet. A little moss is acceptable, but it should not be against the trunk.

1 The tree as it sits in the pot before treatment. Despite this rot the tree looks extremely healthy.

2 Close-up of the damaged area—you can see the space in the trunk at the base.

3 Removing the tree from the pot The trunk is lightly pressed to work out how far the rot may have traveled up the trunk.

4 Examining the rotted area. The orange spot is the fungal development after the rot has occurred. This can be seen at the base when the bonsai has been removed from the pot.

5 Cutting out the rot using an electric router and narrow round head—but you can also use a Dremel–Hobby carving tool.

6 The area after the rot is cut out. Simply brush or use a blower to remove the dust.

7 Treating the area with lime sulfur. This goes on yellow but dries off white. Apply one coat now, another in a week's time, and a further coat a week later. Repeat each year at least once.

8 Repotting the tree in a higher position and replacing the angle of the tree.

9 Tease out the roots and carefully search for any root rot. If you find any, remove it to expose the living tissue. Trim the long roots and seal all cuts. Do not use rooting hormone powder with a fungicide as this will damage the beneficial mycelium.

10 The tree has a good base to stand on, despite having the rotted area removed. The tree is planted higher in the pot, exposing the entire repaired area, the angle is reset, and the foliage tidied. The tree looks fine in its new position.

chapter 4

Styling and Display

WIRING IS THE MEANS BY WHICH YOU CREATE THE SHAPE OF YOUR BONSAI. THE WIRE GOES ON AND, ONCE THE TREE HAS SET INTO ITS NEW SHAPE, THE WIRING IS CUT AWAY AND REMOVED.

Wiring and shaping

The bonsai being wired in the picture (right) is a Japanese trident, (*Acer buergerianum*). Large tridents are easily grown in warmer areas in North America. I saw good examples in Alabama and I am sure that many nurseries will have this kind of material available. Chinese tridents are often imported from Korea.

The first thing is to shorten the branches slightly and then detail wire into the rough shape. As the tree has little structure you have to give it a plan. Later, as the branches develop, you will find that your new branches are in perfect proportion.

Wire comes in a number of thicknesses and you need a variety of these. The easiest wire to use is anodized aluminum, preferably in a brown or copper color. True copper wire is stronger and less resilient. The thing to remember with copper wire is that it starts off as annealed copper wire and is therefore soft, but as soon as you start bending it the wire will change its molecular structure and stiffen. The benefit is that you do not need to use such thick wires and, as the copper becomes stiff, it will hold the branch much more firmly.

Wiring techniques

Branch wiring

Good wiring will control the direction of growth. Use thick, rather than thin wire for this purpose. Apply the wire at a 45° angle, lightly touching the branch firmly applying it without allowing it to bite into the wood. If the wire is applied too tightly the branch will grow into the wire and cause wire marks, or prove impossible to remove later without damage. Wire to the tip of each branch in all cases.

△ Hold wire from behind as you wire

Heavy branch wiring and protection

When wiring two branches, always make sure the lower one is stronger than the upper one if the latter needs to be pulled down. Apply the wire around both, but slip in protection pads on each branch to stop damage. Insert a small pencil, piece of thicker wire, or twig and twist the wires. As they tighten, the upper branch is pulled down.

To protect branches from damage before they are bent, raffia soaked in cold water is used because it is strong and more

△ Raffia is used to prevent damage to the branch during the shaping process

protective. Heavy branch wiring can bend really large branches, from circumferences of 1 inch (2.5 centimeters) and up to 6 inches (15 centimeters).

Apex wiring

Wiring the apex into shape is the most delicate part of the wiring process.

△ The apex of a Beuvronensis pine

Multiple wiring

This technique was developed to reduce the time it takes to wire branches. While very easy for beginners, it is not a traditional method of wiring. However, it does reduce the effort needed by around 50 percent. I watched my own teacher use two thin wires and sometimes three in order to reduce the need to use thick wire. Because two wires are slightly stronger than one, it gives more control. I extended that to using up to 10 wires, which act like a thick wire, with the advantage that there is the opportunity to spur some wire off onto twigs and other branches. Multiple wiring is only used on younger material or initial styling of a tree. Finer wiring is used on more mature or trees in their final styling.

1 Secure the wires onto another branch or a dead stump.

2 Wind the wire together as one wire.

3 As you come along the branch you can now spur off onto the secondary branches easily and wire to the tips of every twig.

4 Always keep the wires together until you spur off so the wiring will look neat. Cut off the excess wire at the tips, or if a small length, just bend in.

5 Use the thinner wires wire at the tips of each small twig as you come to them. Never throttle the twigs or branches as wire will bite into a growing tree. Just touch the edges of the branch.

6 Now you can easily shape and design the bonsai.

How long to retain the wire?

On young trees of no more than three months old, check after six weeks to make sure that the wire is not biting in. Wire will need to be removed from places of vigorous growth. These are the top, or apex, and the ends, or tips, of the branches.

With older or mature trees, the crucial area to watch is the apex and the tips of branches. Check after four weeks and continue to check every week. The species will determine the length of time wire stays on. Very slow-growing trees, such as junipers, have, conversely, fast-growing foliage. However, the trunk and branches grow more slowly, so wire may possibly be left on for six months in temperate climates, but will need to be removed in warmer areas. Faster-growing trees, such as maples

(*Acer*), will need constant checking after three weeks. Remove the wire as soon as you see the branches expanding into it.

Generally speaking, though, three months is the guideline for leaving wire.

I have seen many new buds and soft bark destroyed by wire being unwound rather than cut. The best way is to cut the wire carefully from the entire branch, as that does not damage the tree. While wire per unit is costly, you do get a lot of it for your money, so, when you are cutting off the wire, remember that you are also preserving essential parts of your bonsai.

△ Always remove wire by cutting off rather than unwiring. Unwinding will damage the bark, new buds, and young growth

Designing a collected olive, *Olea europea*

Artist: Salvatore Liporace, Milan.

The design period was three years, from initial styling.

1 This is an old collected olive, in a pot for a number of years. It is 30 inches (75 centimeters) tall. Salvatore Liporace applied a metal branch bender to form the lower branch.

2 Light pruning prior to wiring. The olive has a hard wood and is difficult to shape. This tree has a double trunk and good *nebari* (surface roots).

3 After initial training and wiring, it is now time to get it out of the old plastic pot. The roots are healthy.

4 The first pot is a soft-edged rectangle in green.

5 There are some very heavy, thick, downward roots and these need to be removed prior to potting. Cut paste (or Kiyonal wound sealer) is always applied to open cuts on the roots to protect them from disease or insect attack.

6 The tree is now in its first pot. This pot, while attractive, was too formal and the color was too much like the leaves. This was visually unsatisfactory. Pots should enhance the overall image and not take over the show.

7 The tree, two years later, is now in its final form. Liporace decided that the tree needed a newer front and the olive was turned accordingly. The new pot is by the German potter, Peter Krebs. The branches have been wired down and the image is now lighter and more delicate. It is now a bonsai.

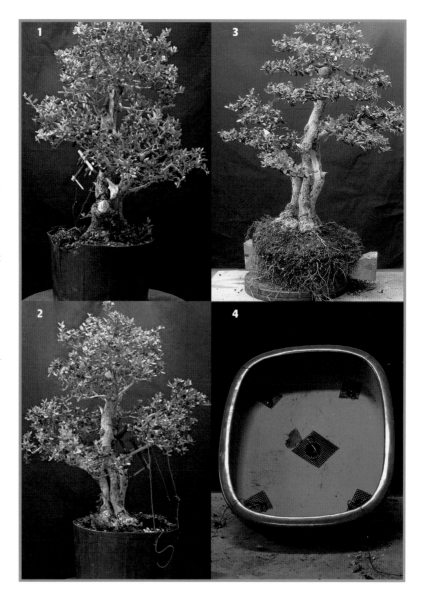

Pine styling in four years

Artist: Salvatore Liporace

1 The original tree was very rough and 36 inches (91 centimeters) tall.

2 Basic styling was required to find the "line" of the tree.

3 After the shaping of the tree, a few months later it is looking more like a bonsai.

4 The following year the tree is now becoming denser. The branches look more natural, and require some pruning.

5 The result of the pruning are allowed to grow back.

6 The finished shape of the tree is starting to develop with more branch pruning and shaping.

7 The finished bonsai, four years from the star of training.

Juniperus chinensis — "Old Gold"

Artist: Luigi Maggione

Luigi Maggione from Milan, a student of Salvatore Liporace, won the International Ben Oki Award set up by Bonsai Clubs International. His entry was this *Juniperus* "Old Gold," 14-year-old material grown in a container for a further three years to develop a good root mass and to ensure health and vigor.

1 First basic plan was to remove some of the foliage not required and establish the jinned areas. Apex of jinn was created, as were the lower twin branches, and the second lower branch.

2 A plan for the *shari* was lightly sketched on the trunk before making the final decision.. Some of the bark was removed exposing the trunk to simulate great age or *shari*. Rough wiring to establish the general shape was also done.

3 Finer wiring was now attended to. The trunk was cleaned at this stage and some more bark was removed to show lifelines as in a very old tree.

4 After the tree was completed it was left to settle for a further year. Some refinement work went on during this period. A year later it was transferred into a training (temporary) pot. Further work was done to increase the density of the foliage by plucking and heavy feeding.

▷ The following year the tree was transferred into its final pot and refined. It should be noted that Milan enjoys a temperate climate and has two growing seasons. The speed of growth may not be as much in cooler regions.

Carving and shaping

This is the method used to achieve aged bonsai in relatively young trees. Sometimes, electrical tools are used because they remove wood very quickly. Many newcomers are not interested in carving when they start, but wish to know simple techniques such as jinning, or how to create dead branches or tips of trees and maybe *shari*, the dead wood on the trunk.

△ A view of Bryce Canyon in Utah, showing the twisted stump of a tree. Images like this show us how to create natural-looking shapes

▷ Carving a trunk with a side cutter or angle cutter. The wood is stroked in a downward motion—never up or across

Improving the look of a bonsai

Preparing your trees for display

1 Carefully remove a very shallow section of the top soil and old moss without damaging the roots.

2 Cut any old or visible dead roots or thin crossing roots (crossing over other roots) or reset them into a better position if possible.

3 Replace the top soil with a light mix, such as Akadama or grit. Otherwise add fresh soil as used in the pot already.

4 Brush the excess away from the trunk.

5 Rub a little olive oil on the tray and rub well in to clean up the color. Always wipe the tray down with a damp cloth prior to doing this.

6 If displaying a smooth trunk tree, such as this yew, apply a little olive oil to the trunk with a brush. Then rub in the oil with a cloth to bring out the color.

Presenting bonsai for display

Cleaning the trunk

This is a dead area created to look like an old tree. It is a yew. However, it has become dirty and needs to have some fresh lime sulfur applied.

1 Brush the dirt carefully from the area—I use a soft wire brush.

2 You can apply Jin Seal or lime sulfur to preserve and whiten dead wood areas

3 Mix the lime sulfur with a little black ink to give a gray color rather than a bright white, which can look contrived.

Cleaning the soil surface

If you wish to display your bonsai, you first need to tidy up the surface of the soil. Removing weeds and planting some moss will allow the tree to be seen in the best possible light.

Plain finish

1 Carefully remove the weeds in the pot, trying not to take the root as well the weed. Carefully pull the weed. If it is stiff, use a chopstick— gently—to loosen the soil around the weed.

2 Fill holes created in the soil with fresh soil and tamp down.

3 Finally, brush the surface to even it out. (I have used Akadama as a top dressing).

Moss finish

If you have an untidy surface you can clean and improve it by applying moss and top dressing. First remove the weeds and then apply a top dressing. Apply the moss in such a way as to emulate grassy mounds around a large tree.

Remember to remove moss in the winter because it can harbor pests. Also, protect moss in the spring, because the birds use it for nests—as well as trying to find those pests under it that you forgot to expose!

Cleaning the pot

This is important if you wish to exhibit either at home or at a show of some kind. A dirty pot looks untidy and detracts from the bonsai.

1 Wipe the pot with a cloth to remove dirt or dust. Apply oil (olive oil or very light machine oil) with a brush taking care not to let any get into the soil.

2 Rub in the oil with a cloth to achieve a clean polished finish.

Traditional styles of bonsai

There are many styles of bonsai and all refer to natural styles in nature. Many have Japanese names such as *fukinagashi, chokkan, nebari,* and *shari.* These are terms that work in the same way as Latin nomenclature works with garden plants.

Once you get to know the words, no matter what language you speak, any fellow bonsai enthusiast will understand what you mean. John Yoshio Naka, the great Japanese American teacher and authority on styles and size definitions, identified both the major styles and heights. Here are some examples of bonsai styles as well as natural trees.

▷ Formal upright yew, collected from an old yew hedge, slanted–or *Moyogi-shakan* yew (*Taxus cuspidata*), ten-year old material prior to styling. 20" (50 cm) high.

1 *Moyogi*–Informal upright
2 *Soju*–Twin Trunk
3 *Ishi*–Zuke Root over rock

Japanese term	English meaning	Alternative terms
Chokkan	Formal, upright, no curves or bends in trunk	Straight trunk
Moyogi	Informal, upright, trunk changing direction	
Shakan	Slanted	
Sho-shakan	Small slant	
Chu-shakan	Medium slant	
Dai-shakan	Extreme slant	
Hankan	Very coiled trunk	
Fukinagashi	Windswept	
Bankan	Old coiled trunk	
Saba kan	Hollow trunk	Trunk with a split
Shari kan	Exposed deadwood on the trunk— *shari miki* dead wood with dead branch stumps, also known as "fish bones"	Stickle back, driftwood
Neijikan	Twisted-in-wind trunk and/or branches	
Kobukan	Lumpy trunk, gnarled with age	
Kengai	Cascade	Below pot base
Han kengai	Semi-cascade	Above pot base
Dai kengai	Straight cascade, extreme or long.	Below pot base
Gaito kengai	A tree that is on the edge and cascades with a round *ju-shin* (apex)	Any length
Taki kengai	A cascade changing direction	Waterfall
Ito kengai	Multiple thin cascades	
Takan kengai	Twin or more trunks cascade	Any length
Netsuranari	Raft style from roots	
Ikada	Raft style of trees from fallen trunk	
Ikadabuki	Raft style from a fallen tree, branches take root	
Soju	Twin trunks	
Sokan	Two trunks of differing size from single root	Mother and child
Yose-uye	Forest style	group
Tako zukuri	Octopus style—very twisted branches and trunk	Old style
Ishi-zuke	Root over rock	Rock clinging
Ne-agari	Exposed root style-erosion exposed roots	
Hoki dachi	Broom style. Fan shape with even growth	
Bunjin	Literati—similar to elegant sumi paintings: long Trunk with slight growth at top. Not heavy.	Freestyle

1 *Bonkei* or landscape with figures

2 *Uro* or trunk hole

Japanese term	English term	Alternative terms
Ara-kawacho	Rough bark	
Mastu (mats)	Pine bonsai	
Ju shin	Top of a bonsai tree	Apex, crown
Shoki	Collected bonsai that is established	
Yamadori	Collected natural material for bonsai or natural bonsai not yet refined into a bonsai	
Tangei	Bonsai material or material good for making bonsai	Potensai
Bonsai	A tree in a tray or container	
Bonkei	Landscapes with other plants, animals figures, buildings, etc	
Bonseki bonsekei	Landscape planting but no figures only rocks, moss and trees	Saikei
Bonju	Bonsai tree	
Uro	Hole in trunk with healed edges	
Nebari*	Surface roots	
Saba miki	Split trunk	
Shari kan	Bark split from trunk	
Shari*	Exposed areas on trunk	Shari miki
Jin,* jinning	Exposed areas on branches or tips	Jinn
Dai	Table to display a bonsai	
Daiza	Shaped table or a base for a *suiseki*	

* important and common terms

3 *Shari* and Jinn. Dead wood areas on trunk and branches. Created to make the bonsai look old. *Moyogi Dai Shakan.* Informal upright with extreme slant.

4 *Yamadori.* Collected material from Water cypress (*Taxodium*)

5 *Bonsekei*–or landscape without figures and with moss, sand or rocks

Japanese name	English name	Latin name
Momji or kaede	Maple	Acer
Sugi	Japanese cedar	Cryptomeria
Keyaki	Japanese gray bark elm	Zelkova serrata
Ichijiku	Fig	Ficus
Shide or soro	Hornbeam	Carpinus
Goyo-matsu (mats)	Five-needle white pine (also *Pinus pentaphylla*)	Pinus parviflora
Kuro-matsu (mats)	Japanese black pine, two needles	Pinus thunbergii
Shimpaku	Juniper (the most popular juniper grown as bonsai)	Juniperus chinensis var. sargentii
Kashu shimpaku	California juniper; also Utah and other similar species such as western juniper and common juniper (*Juniperus communis*)	J. californica J. osteosperma J. occidentalis
Benishitan	Cotoneaster	Cotoneaster
Botangi	Buttonwood; silver buttonwood; from warmer climes in America	Conocarpus erectus sericeus
Kashi, kunugi	Oak; many varieties	Quercus
Maki	Podocarpus pine	Podocarpus
Satsuki	Flowering azalea; kurume azaleas	Rhododendron azalea
Ezo-matsu	Spruce, Japanese; jezo, ezo or yezo spruce	Picea jezoensis
Ichii	Yew: Japanese, American, or English	taxus
Sarusuberi	Crepe myrtle	Lagerstroemia indica
Tsuge	Box; stiff when old but great for bonsai	Buxus

1 *Shimpaku* or *Juniperus chinensis* scale foliage

2 *Kuro Matsu*-Japanese Black pine *Moyogi*

3 *Ichijiku*, Wellington fig. Close up of unusual surface root or *nebari*

4 *Ficus wellingtonia*

5 *Shohin* or mini bonsai. Japanese Black pine-*Kuro Matsu*

Styling class

Style: Yose-uye, group or forest style from nursery stock

Joe Day in Alabama has a very large collection of Trident maple *(Acer buergerianum)* stock with which I could make a forest style group or *yose-uye*. Joe is not only enthusiastic about forest style, but also makes slate bases, and I used one of these for this example. I want to show a double forest group illustrating perspective planting, that is, a near-view forest and a far-view forest. To do this, I simply made a smaller forest that looks as if it were in the far distance. Set slightly back from the bigger group, it gives the illusion of perspective. I created a formal upright group called *chokkan yose-uye* rather than any other style because the material is young, very sparse, and straight.

△ Trident maple stock   △ Slate bases

1 The slate is about 3 feet (1 meter) long. Joe and I drilled holes in the base for the retaining wires. Slate or the alternative, fiberglass resin, is easy to drill.

2 The retaining wires were put into place all over the container.

3 We built a small wall of peat muck, which is a 50:50 mix of long-grain peat and clay. They are blended together by hand and then a long sausage is formed and put around the edge of the base to stop the soil from falling out. We have placed the first and biggest tree into place for the larger group.

4 We completed the group by surrounding the main tree with progressively smaller trees to form the outline image of a forest. One tip in making forests is to make sure that no trunk crosses another completely either at the front or the side of the planting.

The smaller group is almost a mirror image of the bigger group but placed slightly back. This gives the impression of a forest away in the distance. It is this illusionary technique that illustrates what bonsai is really about.

Bonsai heights and names

Bonsai come in a variety of heights, from 1 inch (2.5 centimeters) up to 6 feet (1.8 meters). Essentially, the larger bonsai are known as garden bonsai or yard trees, while most bonsai are around a maximum of 40 inches (1.2 meters). Nothing is fixed as to what is and is not bonsai, however, and this size chart is a guideline.

Sizes are measured from soil level to the apex.

Height	Name	English term
1" (2.5 cm)	Keishi tsubo	Thimble size
1–3" (2.5–7.6 cm)	Shito	Mini size—very small
3–6" (7.6–15.2 cm)	Mame	Mini size
6–8" (15.2–20.3 cm)	Shohin	Katade—small size
8–16" (20.3–40.6 cm)	Kifu	Sho—small to medium size
16–24" (40.6 –61 cm)	Chu	Medium size
24–40" (61–101 cm)	Dai	large size

▽ A selection of popular indoor bonsai styles and sizes. 5" to 20" (12 to 50 cm).

How to view a bonsai

Front or back?

When bonsai are made there is generally a favored viewing angle. Sometimes called the "front," this is the starting point for a bonsai. Of course, a normal tree does not have a front and anyone looking at that tree will have a different angle than another person.

However, while we need a front there should also be a back, a right, a left, and a top (that enables you to look down through the foliage to make sure the branches are not covering each other completely), a surface root image, and of course the hidden "view": a good underground root system.

△ Front view   △ Back view   △ Left view   △ Right view

A well-designed and styled bonsai must be appealing viewed from any angle

chapter 5

Easy Species Guide

I HAVE CHOSEN A NUMBER OF RELATIVELY EASY AND POPULAR BONSAI SPECIES TO HELP YOU START A COLLECTION. THE RESULTS SHOWN HERE TOOK BETWEEN FIVE AND TEN YEARS TO ACHIEVE.

Of all the bonsai grown around the world, two species are most desired. The first is pine and the second, maple. In some countries it is too warm for pines and too cold for maples, but in many countries I find that bonsai enthusiasts still try their best to keep these two trees.

In this chapter I have chosen pine and maple to demonstrate the different techniques required in growing and to discuss their general care needs. The techniques can be applied to many species. Evergreen conifers, deciduous species and further common species, with descriptions and cultivation information, have all been included

Pine

Suitable species *Pinus parviflora or Pinus pentaphylla, Pinus sylvestris*

White pine bonsai (*Pinus parviflora*) are the most popular bonsai sold to beginners. Also known as *Pinus pentaphylla*, they come from China, Japan, Korea, Israel, and the Pacific Rim area.

Despite the huge number of varieties, or cultivars, of White pine, all have a white stomatic band down the middle of the needle (or leaf). The tree, or shrub, in its original state is a blue–green color but cultivars can be any color from green to bright yellow.

The needles are between 2 and 3 inches long (or 5–7.5 centimeters). The cones, which are formed from the flowers, are

△ Large White pine, 46" (115 cm) high and over 100 years old

around 3 to 5 inches (7.5–12.5 centimeters) long, are conical in shape, and can be in clusters or singles. In bonsai cultivation, we can reduce the needles to a size smaller than half an inch (1 centimeter), although the normal size is about one inch (2.5 centimeters).

They are styled very simply with a twist or two on the trunk and are usually grafted onto the stronger Black pine base. Some varieties have short needle clusters and some have very dense needle clusters. The difference between White pine and other pine species is that the white pine has a cluster of five needles around each bud. The Scots, Red, and Black pines have clusters of two and some varieties of red have clusters of three.

Its natural growth habit is low and conical when young but flat-topped and spreading when the tree is mature. As a bonsai, it can be any shape, with the common style being pyramidal with the branches in clearly defined steps up to the apex. This gives the image of a younger tree and as a bonsai it is much more attractive to the viewer.

Pine should be kept out of extreme weather conditions —wind,

▽ Scots pine (*Pinus sylvestris*). The tree is nearly 400 years old. Images such as these inspire bonsai artists

△ White pine *(Pinus pentaphylla)* is 42" (107 cm) high and 39" (99 cm) wide, and has been in training for 50 years. There is a weakness at one side and too much growth at the other, so it needs balancing

rain, and sun, and centrally heated homes. Many bonsai die within a few weeks of purchase if they are not kept correctly. If this happens, it can be annoying and expensive.

Put the tree in a slightly shaded place and spray lightly every day for the first 14 days. After that time, give the tree about four hours' sun per day, but still find a place for it away from high winds.

It is wise not to feed immediately you have bought a new bonsai. Wait until the tree has settled down. The tree may have been repotted recently and the roots freshly cut. If you feed too soon after purchase, you may damage the roots. Ask when the tree was last repotted. Explain why you need this information. If the seller is not sure, then it is best not to feed the bonsai for about six weeks.

If you obtain an outdoor bonsai tree in the winter, do not bring it into a centrally heated house. This will accelerate the normal growing period of the tree, exhausting it and drying up the needles.

Watering

Pines need semidry conditions in the winter and the soil kept slightly damp in the growing season. Pine bonsai do not like very wet conditions. Spray the needles only from summer to early fall, but in both the morning and late evening. (See the care charts' sections on soil and feeding on pages 34-37.)

Needle reduction

To reduce needles on established trees, start to withhold water as the buds develop. This makes the needles smaller. When the buds have set and the needles open, resume normal watering. This is not appropriate for young trees, as they need vigor to develop.

Pests and diseases

- Aphids, adelgids, mealy bug, red spider mite, and *Lophodermium pinastre* (pine-needle cast).
- If pests arrive, treat with systemic insecticide.
- Lopho is a fungus identified by lateral yellow stripes on the needle and is treated weekly with a copper fungicide for five or six weeks. When using any fungicide on a pine, do not allow the fungicide to get onto the soil because it will damage the beneficial mycelium that helps the pine roots to grow. Cover it with a polythene sheet or plastic bag and then a towel.
- Adelgids look like a woolly fluff between the needles. Systemic insecticide will kill the insect but use a concentrated hose spray to wash away the fluff.

Feeding

- Always use bought fertilizers at half strength.
- For young trees in the spring, feed with a high-nitrogen fertilizer; in summer, with a balanced fertilizer; and in early autumn, with a low-nitrogen fertilizer. Feed every three weeks at the beginning of the season and every four weeks by early summer through to the end of autumn. (See the care charts on pages 34-37.)
- On established trees, using fertilizers at full strength is particularly dangerous, because the roots are very tender and may suffer from being fed. You do not want lush juvenile growth, so feed until early summer with low-nitrogen fertilizer. Give balanced feed in summer and in the fall feed with low-nitrogen fertilizer again.
- Feed mature trees about every five weeks using slow-release fertilizer pellets, such as Bio Gold. Mature trees need just enough feed to replace lost nutrients in the soil. Feeding trace elements to all bonsai is necessary, but, since most proprietary food have these in the formula, it is unnecessary to add more. Check the pack.

Pruning

- Every three years, prune the two-year-old needles on young trees, and three-year-old needles on mature trees at the rear of each bud needle cluster. Do not trim the needles nearest the new buds. Cut the needles above the tiny sheath. Doing this encourages new buds to develop on the older wood.
- Leave only two or three buds at each tip, depending on the health of the tree.

◁ Cut the needles above the tiny sheath

out 50 percent of the candle with your fingers by holding the bottom of the candle to stop it from being broken off the tree, and pull the rest with your other hand. Leave all obviously weak buds alone and, if the branch has *only* weak buds, wait until they have swollen. However, if this has not occurred by late spring, then simply proceed with the other branches. ▽

- If you wish to develop young inner buds along the branch, then prune out some of the leading tips that are not required.
- Start cutting candles (buds) from the top of the tree by half to two-thirds, each week. Work your way down until you reach the bottom layer of branches. (White pine only).
- The strongest bud at the top of the tree will grow.
- Do not prune all the buds on the tree at the same time, because this will exhaust the tree.
- Every three years it is better to pull the soft new needles out from the sheath, as this forces the tree to create shorter needles the following year.

- A week later, pluck the next layer of branches in the same way and work your way up to what will be by now a vigorous top area. Using both hands, hold the base of the bud and pluck off 50 percent of the candle bud. ▽

Two-needle pines

Scots pine *(Pinus sylvestris)*. When these trees are either collected or bought in garden centers, they invariably have long branches with little or no twig structure. The technique for back budding in order to develop twigs is quite straightforward.

- From mid-spring the tree grows candles. Starting at the bottom of the tree, or the weaker lower branches, pluck

- The reason you pluck off the candles in stage, from the base upward is that the stronger growth is at the top of the tree. Should you start to pluck from the top, all the tree's energy would be needed to repair the damage and would bypass weaker areas. This could result in eventual loss within the weaker areas.
- The next thing to look out for is the formation of twin buds.
- Pluck the longer bud and wait until the smaller bud has grown longer than the plucked bud...
- ...then remove the first bud and...
- ...reduce the new bud by half but in the same weekly regime.
- At no time leave more than two buds on any growth point.
- You must reduce this multiple growth to the one or two buds if they are important to your overall plan.
- After these new buds have developed, keep the end of that branch short, or else the sap will bypass the new bud to feed the stronger bud.
- You can remove the entire leader bud if you have strong back buds, but be very careful: if these buds are weak, you will lose the entire branch or twig if you remove the leader.

This method differs from that for the White pine, with which you begin at the top and work your way down. The tree is less likely to abort its weaker, lower branches. The white pine has a very specialized series of auxin channels (auxin is a plant growth hormone) that require the stronger buds to be trimmed first.

The new growth is much softer than in the case of two-needle pines. Unlike these, the five-needle pines can be pruned back quite hard after the needles have broken. If you feel the difference between the needle varieties you will see what I mean.

Established trees

If you have established the tree and reduced the needles, then you can remove 75 percent of the length of the candles to maintain and build dense pads. This also applies to White pine (Pinus parviflora). You will see that your tree starts to shape up over the next three or four years.

- Look at the inner buds on each branch and, when bud plucking starts, pluck the inner buds first.
- Five days later do the outer buds.
- Start on the next upper layer a week later.
- Although this does increase the actual plucking time by 75 percent, you will soon see the difference.
- Maintenance pruning of buds is done when the tree has been relatively completed. This means reverting to the basic plucking procedure. Work on one layer of branches at a time, covering all the buds at the same time on each layer, and progressing each week upward.

Soil type

- A free-draining soil is important for all pines and should be five parts of grit to three parts organic, such as a mixture of peat, leaf mold, or composted bark.

- Speak to the seller of the bonsai or to other growers in your area and they will advise you on the best soil component for your climate.

- Trees in hotter climates may need a little more organic matter to retain moisture than do trees in colder or wetter climates.

- If you have access to Japanese soils, you can mix 50 percent Akadama with 50 percent Kureyu Pine Soil for fast drainage to avoid sodden conditions.

- Repot every three years for young trees and every five years for mature trees.

- Use rust, brown, gray, or deep-blue pots for pines.

Light/shade requirements

- Pines like some shade for part of the day in the summer.

- A light area free from winter climatic problems during the cold months.

- Full sun will make the tree more yellow in most cases, while full shade (not advised) will force the glaucous, blue-green color to come out.

- Blend the light requirements and you will have a healthy tree.

△ Ponderosa pines and junipers − Red Rock Canyon, Utah

Maples

△ **Kashima maple**

Maples are one of the most popular species for bonsai all over the world. While it is not always possible to keep maples in some climates, they still account for the majority of bonsai in temperate areas.

The finely twigged structure in winter is magnificent and entirely indicative of a full-sized tree. The spring and autumn foliage is magnificent and very colorful. The dense summer foliage again mirrors a full-sized tree and is one of the reasons people choose maples.

Although the red-leaf cultivars, such as "Deshojo" and "Seigen," are the prettiest because of the color of their leaf

through the year, I suggest you begin with the hardier green-leafed types such as pure Japanese maple *(Acer palmatum)*, and Trident maple *(Acer buergerianum)*.

The cultivars or "Yatsubusa" varieties are more delicate so do not leaf-prune these types unless you are sure that they can take it. *Acer atropurpurae,* the maple with the dark, plum-colored leaf, is sometimes weak and not easy to back-bud. Do not leaf-prune this color group. You develop this variety through bud pinching. Pinching is discussed later.

"Kiyohime" are very dense but they are very strong at the sides, so keep the side growth down, or the upper portion will die back.

Many deciduous trees such as maples will suffer leaf burn if you put them out into windy weather such as in springtime. The time to put them out is when the soft leaf becomes firm and hard. Keep them in a sheltered area away from wind if possible. You may have to build a simple shelter.

Watering

Water to keep the soil damp. Plants will need less water in winter in a cold or temperate climate, but if you live in a humid area then Trident maples *(Acer buergerianum)* will possibly need regular watering until you force the leaf fall by cutting all the leaves off. Reduce water slightly in this case, because the tree is unable to transpire through the leaves until the new leaves have set. Mist-spray once a day during spring and twice a day during summer, but do that in the morning and in the early evening. In the fall, mist-spray once a day until the leaves start to turn. Do not waterlog, though—a light misting once a day to increase humidity in the leaves and soil (see care charts in chapter 3) is enough.

Pests

Everything goes for deciduous trees! However, the most common problems are aphids, whitefly, blackfly, and, depending on your area, caterpillars. (Although caterpillars are usually species-specific, some are just hungry.) Treatment is a systemic preparation in most cases. Spraying directly onto leaves may damage maples, although some new pesticides have come onto the market recently that do not damage leaves. Ask in your local bonsai nursery.

Feeding

The care charts in chapter 3 cover this, and here are the salient points.

Developing maple bonsai—young to mid-stage

- Feed when the leaves are open.
- Feed zero- or very low-nitrogen fertilizer during the lush soft stage of growth.
- When the leaves start to harden then increase the nitrogen.
- Reduce in hot summer months to zero feed, because the trees are less able to take it up.
- After the peak, begin feeding with low-nitrogen fertilizer, because that builds strength in the wood.
- Do not feed when the leaves fall.

△ Kashima maple

Mature maples

If you want good color in the autumn, then you need to use a pellet food, or indeed stop nitrogen completely, because that stops the bright color changes.

Pruning and ramification

The health of the tree depends on your ability to create more and more twigs, which of course hold the leaves that allow the tree to breathe. This is called ramification. It just means creating dense, fine twig structure.

The health advantages of more twigs and branches are that increasingly fine root development takes place and the tree has a solid base to stand on. Roots also help define twigs. Roots mirror the branches and twigs.

The value of a tree with plenty of fine twigs, buds, branches, and roots advertises your artistic ability as a grower of miniature trees. The appearance of a finely twigged deciduous bonsai (or a dense pine) gives you a feeling of satisfaction.

Main buds at the end of each branch

- The next thing to be aware of is that, when new back buds have developed, keep the end of that branch short, or else the sap will bypass the new bud to feed the strongest bud.
- To get smaller leaves, pluck out the center of the buds as they start to form.
- If you leave it too late, you cannot create the above effect.
- During spring, you can continue to pluck out the center buds on the branches you are happy with as far as length is concerned. This, in turn, helps to develop fine twigs.

Light and shade

If you keep the tree in shade, the branches and twigs will grow very long between the internodes or leaf stalks. This is fine for young trees, but not for mature ones. If you grow in bright light and not direct hot sun, the internodes will be short.

▽ A beautiful maple in leaf

Mountain maple *(Acer palmatum)*

**Height: 42" (105 cm) • Width of trunk:
6" (15 cm) • Years in training: 11**

Cut down from a full-sized tree, the branches were grown from the bare trunk. During a severe frost four years prior to this photograph, I lost one side of the tree, but managed to get the growth back on one side. Part of the trunk, though dead, is now preserved with the back section taking the form.

For full maple care, see pages 84–86.

WATERING: Once a week in winter or just keep the soil damp; once a day in spring; twice a day in summer; and once a day in autumn.

FREE-DRAINING SOIL: 60 percent grit, 40 percent organic

FEEDING: High nitrogen in spring and low-nitrogen feed in late summer. None in midsummer.

PLACEMENT: Bright area. Likes sun but watch for drying.

PRUNING AND PINCHING: General pruning to remove twigs growing in wrong direction.

Juniper *(Juniperus chinensis)*

**Height: 30" (75 cm) • Width: 28" (70 cm) •
Years in training: 8**

The various species of juniper are very easy to care
for if you remember to keep pinching the foliage.

WATERING: once a week in winter or just keep the
soil damp; once a day in spring; twice a day in
summer; and once a day in autumn.

FREE-DRAINING SOIL: 60 percent grit, 30
percent organic or Akadama, 10 percent
chopped-up long-grain moss.

FEEDING: Feed at half strength through the spring
to autumn period. Reduce in midsummer.

PLACEMENT: Needs some sun and fresh
movement of air because of the dense foliage.
Shade brings out the darker coloration but too
much will cause the tree to grow to length on
the branches.

PRUNING AND PINCHING: Pinching means nipping
out the end of the growth two or three times a year
with your fingers. Do not twist the fingers, since that
will tear the foliage and it will become brown.
However, all light pruning requires you to mist the
foliage during and after pruning or pinching to keep
up the humidity. That, in turn, reduces any die-back
of foliage. Careful cutting of tips is fine but spray foliage
after this to reduce browning.

Larch *(Larix decidua)*

Height: 44" (110 cm) • Width: 36" (90 cm) • Years in training: 8

Like one or two other conifers, larch *(Larix)* is actually a
deciduous genus of the pine family. There are many species,
such as European larch *(Larix decidua),* and most are easy for
bonsai cultivation. Grown throughout the northern regions of the
USA and into Canada, this is a good tree to start as a single tree
or as a group. This example has been planted in a handmade
Japanese pot.

△ A close up of larch foliage

▷ Formal upright European larch. 39" (95 cm) in height, 40 years old and ten years
in training

WATERING: Once a week in winter or just keep the soil damp;
once a day in spring; twice a day in summer; and once a day
in autumn.

FREE-DRAINING SOIL: 60 percent grit, 40 percent organic (or
50:50 Akadama and Kureyu).

FEEDING: Only after needles come out. High-nitrogen feed in
spring, balanced feed in early summer. Stop in midsummer
and use low-nitrogen feed in autumn.

PLACEMENT: Must have good air circulation. Choose a bright spot
but allow some shade in hot sun. Does not like humid areas.

PRUNING AND PINCHING: When you are developing larch
bonsai, allow the shoots to grow through the season without
cutting. Cut back only to the last two buds in the midwinter
or early spring prior to the buds' swelling. Remove the bud
that is growing in the wrong direction. This process will take
you around five years. On mature trees you can prune the
summer foliage back or leave it to fill in certain areas of your
design. Wire in winter or midsummer.

Western hemlock *(Tsuga heterophylla)*

Height: 34" (85 cm) • Width: 48" (120 cm) • Years in training: 4

This conifer, a native of North America, is normally grown as a timber tree. It is excellent for bonsai, because it shapes easily and its soft outline is very attractive. This particular tree is in Island forest style.

WATERING: Once a week in winter, or just keep the soil damp; once a day in spring; twice a day in summer; and once a day in autumn.

FREE-DRAINING SOIL: 60 percent grit, 40 percent organic (or 50:50 Akadama and Kureyu).

FEEDING: Late spring to early summer with high-nitrogen feed. Late summer to early fall with low-nitrogen feed.

PLACEMENT: Needs fresh, circulating air, a light spot, some sun.

PRUNING AND PINCHING: Prune mass in midsummer. Wire at this time.

Boulevard cypress *(Chamaecyparus pisifera)*

Height: 22" (55 cm) • Width: 29" (62 cm) • Years in training: 25

This is easily wired, shaped, and hand-pinched and is suitable for all styles. The trick is to keep it pinched to a tight foliage pad as otherwise it will run away with the shape.

WATERING: Once a week in winter, or just keep the soil damp; once a day in spring; twice a day in summer; and once a day in autumn.

FREE-DRAINING SOIL: 60 percent grit, 40 percent organic (or 50:50 Akadama and Kureyu).

FEEDING: High-nitrogen in spring and low in late summer. None in midsummer.

PLACEMENT: Like most conifers, it needs good air circulation and light.

PRUNING AND PINCHING: Soft foliage is easily cut to shape initially. It will brown a little, and to avoid this, mist three times a day and it will be fine in a couple of weeks.

Honeysuckle *(Lonicera nitida)*

Height: 12" (30 cm) • Width: 20" (50 cm) • Years in training: 10

This is one of the shrub honeysuckles that are used for hedging. Easy to grow from cuttings, they are pruned by trimming with shears and will soon develop into a treelike shape. When small they make excellent mini-size bonsai. They can grow to nine feet (2.7 meters) normally. The trunk is fibrous and sometimes rots out. This can develop into a pleasant feature for a bonsai.

WATERING: Once a week in winter or just keep the soil damp; once a day in spring; twice a day in summer; and once a day in autumn.

FREE-DRAINING SOIL: 60 percent grit, 40 percent organic (or 50:50 Akadama and Kureyu).

FEEDING: Miracle Grow throughout the year for young trees, a high-nitrogen feed in spring, and low-nitrogen in late summer for mature trees. Reduce feed for all mature bonsai as previously described, because that forces the growth. Pellet surface food four times a year is usually adequate.

PLACEMENT: Grows well anywhere. Brighter areas will help all bonsai though.

PRUNING AND PINCHING: Cut with shears any time during the growing season. Koos Le Roux from South Africa simply throws the cuttings onto the ground and they soon take. Pictured below is one of his exquisite landscape plantings.

△ **MIniature honeysuckle (*Lonicera nitada*).** *Bonseki* **by Koos le Roux, South Africa.**

Chinese hackberry *(Celtis sinensis)*

Height: 22" (55 cm) • Width: 18" (45 cm)
• Years in training: 10

Popular as a bonsai around the world, the hackberry, sometimes known as white stinkwood, is very easy to grow. I would suggest that initially you grow it in the garden, or at least in a large growing box, and feed heavily. This will develop bulk in the tree prior to your turning it into a bonsai.

WATERING: Once a week in winter just keep the soil damp; once a day in spring; twice a day in summer; and once a day in autumn. Needs lots of water in summer.

FREE-DRAINING SOIL: 60 percent grit, 40 percent organic (or 50:50 Akadama and Kureyu).

FEEDING: High nitrogen in spring and low in late summer. None in midsummer

PLACEMENT: Bright area. Some shade for pot in midsummer. Grows in most countries and climates.

PRUNING AND PINCHING: Pinch back to the first set of leaves at the top of the tree and the second set at the sides. Keep the trunk as clear from pruning cuts as possible. Likes a deeper container when young to encourage roots.

Japanese Gray Bark elm

(Zelkova serrata)

**Height: 40" (100 cm) • Width: 34" (85 cm)
• Years in training: 10**

This one is grown from cuttings but as a rule it is better to grow in the garden for speed of growth. A growing box will also be adequate. You need to lift it once a year to prune the roots and straighten them out, and let the leader grow wild. It is important to straighten the roots because you also need to keep the trunk as clear of foliage as possible. The beauty is not only in the dense foliage but in the bark. To get tighter foliage, tie the young twigs up into a bunch during the late fall and into early spring when the buds start to swell. Remove any crossing twigs and prune to the first set of leaves at the top, the second set at the sides and the third set at the bottom line.

WATERING: Once a week in winter or just keep the soil damp; once a day in spring; twice a day in summer; and once a day in autumn.

FREE-DRAINING SOIL: 60 percent grit, 40 percent organic (or 50:50 Akadama and Kureyu).

FEEDING: Nitrogen in spring and low nitrogen in late summer. None in midsummer

△ This example of Japanese Gray Bark elm is being developed into a broom style. Repeated cutting is one way of developing multiple twigs but it may just be best to cut the tree right back to the base of the first branch, then seal and wrap with raffia to force the new buds to grow straight

PLACEMENT: Bright area, but keep out of direct sun in hot weather.

PRUNING AND PINCHING: Pinch back to first set of leaves at top of the tree and second set at the sides. Keep trunk as clear from pruning cuts as possible. Likes a deeper container when young to encourage roots. Broom styles are usual for this type of bonsai because of the way it develops fine twigs. It particularly suits a treelike image, such as broom or formal upright. However, you are not limited to this style — any style can be created.

△ Japanese Gray Bark elm in full foliage

chapter 6

Style Gallery

THE GALLERY PRESENTS A VARIETY OF POPULAR BONSAI SPECIES STYLES THAT HAVE BEEN CREATED OVER A TIME FRAME OF FIVE TO 20 YEARS. SOME OF THE BIGGER PINES ARE MUCH OLDER, BUT THEY GIVE AN IDEA OF HOW BONSAI EVENTUALLY DEVELOPS.

I have shown a variety of qualities to explain the varying degrees of styling that are available within this time frame. In all the world there are thousands of trees and I cannot include them all in this book,so what I have done is to select some popular ones. The majority of the bonsai shown are exhibited at the Willowbog Collection or come from my own collections. Others have been contributed by other leading bonsai artists.

Pines

Japanese White pine *(Pinus parviflora)*

Height: 23" (58 cm) • Width: 13" (33 cm) • Years in training: 4

The example shown here was grafted onto black pine root stock 10 years previously.

See page 78 for more information on pines.

△ Black pine

Black pine *(Pinus thunbergii)*

Height: 30" (76 cm) • Width: 28" (71 cm) • Years in training: 6

DESCRIPTION: Long needles, with deep, dark, and sometimes corky bark. European black pine is nearer to Scots pine but with longer needles and a lighter green color.

WATERING: Once a week in winter to just keep the soil slightly damp; once a day in spring; twice a day in summer; and once a day in autumn. Reduce watering in cold and temperate climates to once a day in summer if the tree is mature but keep slightly shaded for at least part of the day if the weather is hot. Such trees do not like hot humid climates.

Red pine *(Pinus densiflora)*

Height: 24" (61 cm) • Width: 15" (38 cm) • Years in training: 10

I had two identical shrubs and kept one as a shrub and made the other into a bonsai. The needles have a tendency to be long in a red pine, like Japanese Black pine, although they can be reduced.

See page 78 for more information on pines

△ Japanese White pine

Shore or Sand pine (*Pinus latifolia* var. *contorta*)

Height: 30" (76 cm) • Width: 39" (99 cm) • Years in training: 6

This tree was trained and wired from a 15 year old collected specimen.

See page 78 for more information on pines

△ Shore or Sand pine

Junipers

Common juniper
(Juniperus communis)

**Height: 25" (64 cm) • Width: 12" (30 cm) •
Years in training: 3**

DESCRIPTION: Found over most of the
northern areas of the northern hemisphere.
Excellent collected material with natural
shari and small needle foliage. A similar
tree is *Juniper rigida* or needle juniper.

WATERING: Once a week in winter or just keep
the soil damp; once a day in spring; twice a
day in summer; and once a day in autumn.

FREE-DRAINING SOIL: 80 percent volcanic
grit, 20 percent organic (or 30 percent
Akadama and 70 percent Kureyu).

FEEDING: High nitrogen in spring and low
nitrogen in late summer. None in
midsummer.

PLACEMENT: Likes both shade and sun,
so move it around, or find an area that
has both.

PRUNING AND PINCHING: Pinch out tips of
foliage to encourage tight growth. Grows in
various shapes in the wild.

Meyers juniper

(Juniperus squamata "Meyeri")

**Height: 48" (122 cm) • Width: 23" (58 cm) •
Years in training: 15**

DESCRIPTION: Blue-green foliage with
white band giving a silver appearance
sometimes. Rusty brown trunk. Usually
upright in growth. This example is meant to
represent a natural looking tree with soft
foliage masses.

WATERING: Once a week in winter or just keep
the soil damp; once a day in spring; twice a
day in summer; and once a day in autumn.

FREE-DRAINING SOIL: 60 percent grit
40 percent organic (or 50:50 Akadama
and Kureyu).

FEEDING: High nitrogen in spring and low
nitrogen in late summer. None in
midsummer.

PLACEMENT: An area that enjoys both sun and
shade is ideal.

PRUNING AND PINCHING: Pinch out tips of
foliage to encourage tight growth.

Blauws juniper

(Juniperus chinensis "Blauws")

Height: 22" (56 cm) • Width: 29" (74 cm) • Years in training: 10

DESCRIPTION: Grown from an upright tree, the trunk was laid flat and the branches wired up into individual trees that were formed into a windswept style. This is therefore called a raft windswept style.

WATERING: Once a week in winter or just keep the soil damp; once a day in spring; twice a day in summer; and once a day in autumn.

FREE-DRAINING SOIL: 60 percent grit, 40 percent organic (or 50:50 Akadama and Kureyu).

FEEDING: Nitrogen in spring and low nitrogen in late summer. None in midsummer.

PLACEMENT: Full light in spring and autumn and shaded in summer from hot sun.

PRUNING AND PINCHING: Pinch out tips of foliage to encourage tight growth. As it reacts well to feeding, make sure that you keep up the pinching throughout the growing season.

Another example is the Shimpaku juniper (Juniperus chinensis "Shimpaku"), *below, which stands 34 inches (86 cm) and 32 inches (81 cm) wide. This tree has been trained for 12 years and requires regular plucking of new growth at the terminals to keep its shape.*

△ *Juniperus* "Bauws", raft-style

Other conifers

Japanese larch *(Larix kaempferi)*

Height: 44" (110 cm) • Length: 48" (120 cm) • Years in training: 15

WATERING: Once a week in winter or just keep the soil damp; once a day in spring; twice a day in summer; and once a day in autumn.

FREE-DRAINING SOIL: 60 percent grit, 40 percent organic (or 50:50 Akadama and Kureyu)

FEEDING: Nitrogen in spring and low nitrogen in late summer. None in midsummer.

PLACEMENT: Bright area.

▽ European larch

△ Larch group created from 15-year old trees collected from deer-browsed area.

European larch *(Larix decidua)*

Height: 36" (51 cm) • Width: 40" (74 cm) • Years in training: 10

WATERING: Once a week in winter or just keep the soil damp; once a day in spring; twice a day in summer; and once a day in autumn.

FREE-DRAINING SOIL: 60 percent grit, 40 percent organic (or 50:50 Akadama and Kureyu).

FEEDING: Nitrogen in spring and low nitrogen in late summer. None in mid summer

Western Red cedar or arborvitae *(Thuja plicata)*

Height: 32" (81 cm) • Width: 20" (51 cm) • Years in training: 2

DESCRIPTION: Flaky bark and glossy green foliage with a slight blue-green underneath the leaves.

WATERING: Once a week in winter or just keep the soil damp; once a day in spring; twice a day in summer; and once a day in autumn.

FREE-DRAINING SOIL: 60 percent grit, 40 percent organic (or 50:50 Akadama and Kureyu).

FEEDING: Nitrogen in spring and low nitrogen in late summer. None in midsummer.

PLACEMENT: An area that enjoys both sun and shade is ideal.

PRUNING AND PINCHING: Takes general pruning well and so is used for hedging in many countries.

▽ Western Red cedar or arborvitae

Not true cedars (Cedrus). Western grows in the forests of the Pacific North West, Idaho and Montana. Another species found in North America is Northern White Cedar (Thuja occidentalis) Northeast America, Lake States, the Appalachian Mountains and southern Canada. Thuja orientalis or Oriental Arborvitae is also commonly found in North America but comes from Korea, Manchuria and northern China. In general treat as for juniper.

Hinoki cypress *(Chamaecyparus obtusa)*

Height: 22" (56 cm) • Width: 22" (56 cm) • Years in training: 3

DESCRIPTION: Flat spatulate leaves that fan out. Usually grafted onto large bases that grow faster than the upper. These can sometimes make huge *nebari*.

WATERING: Once a week in winter or just keep the soil damp; once a day in spring; twice a day in summer; once a day in autumn.

FREE-DRAINING SOIL: 60 percent grit, 40 percent organic (or 50:50 Akadama and Kureyu).

FEEDING: Nitrogen in spring and low nitrogen in late summer. None in midsummer.

PLACEMENT: Shade or sun.

PRUNING AND PINCHING: Nip with fingers only. If you do not prune, the branches will grow too long. However, you can elevate them and bend down the foliage pads to reduce the length.

Although not a native of North America as it was introduced from Japan, Hinoki cypress is naturalized in North America and is a popular choice for bonsai. There is one native Chamaecyparus *– the Atlantic white cedar or* Chamaecyparus thyoides*. This grows mainly in a swamp habitat, from central Maine to South Florida and west toward Mississippi in the narrow coastal belt. There are 130 species worldwide.*

Sawara cypress *(Chamaecyparus pisifera)*

Height: 30" (76 cm) • Width: 14" (36 cm) • Years in training: 15

WATERING: Once a week in winter or just keep the soil damp; once a day in spring; twice a day in summer; once a day in autumn.

FREE-DRAINING SOIL: 80 percent volcanic grit, 20 percent organic (or 30 percent Akadama and 70 percent Kureyu).

FEEDING: High nitrogen in spring and low nitrogen in late summer. None in midsummer.

PLACEMENT: Likes both shade and sun, so move it around a bit, or find an area that has both.

PRUNING AND PINCHING: Pinch out tips of foliage to encourage tight growth.

Sawara cypress ▷

Common or English yew

(Taxus baccata)

Height: 24" (61 cm) • Width: 19" (48 cm)
• Years in training: 4 Collected, approximately 150 years old

DESCRIPTION: Dark-green glossy leaves. Paler underside. This example has trunk and *nebari* surface roots that give the impression of a full size tree.

WATERING: Once a week in winter or just keep the soil damp; once a day in spring; twice a day in summer; once a day in autumn.

FREE-DRAINING SOIL: 60 percent grit, 40 percent organic (or 50:50 Akadama and Kureyu).

FEEDING: Nitrogen in spring and low nitrogen in late summer. Full strength to force foliage. None in midsummer.

PLACEMENT: Keep out of frost.

PRUNING AND PINCHING: Let the foliage grow first before wiring. Wire easily into shape and watch that the wire does not bite. Cut tips to half length of new growth. It back-buds easily on old wood, so keep trunk area clear.

The Japanese yew (Taxus cuspidate) shown here is 37 inches (94 cm) high and 30 inches (76 cm) wide. Collected from a garden center as stock eight years ago for landscaping, the original owner cut out the main trunk leaving four oddly placed trunks. I have styled the tree to disguise this and created a bonsai that is balanced on all sides. It will grow on over the next three years.

△ Japanese yew

△ Another example of an English or Common yew

◁ Blue cedar
▽ Norway spruce

Norway spruce *(Picea abies)*

Height: 37" (94 cm) • Width: 54" (137 cm) • Years in training: 10

DESCRIPTION: Popular species that has reddish brown bark and bright green needles. This example is a group planting.

WATERING: Once a week in winter or just keep the soil damp; once a day in spring; twice a day in summer; once a day in autumn.

FREE-DRAINING SOIL: 60 percent grit, 40 percent organic (or 50:50 Akadama and Kureyu).

FEEDING: Balanced feed throughout the growing season to develop the growth. Nitrogen in spring and low nitrogen in late summer. None in midsummer.

PLACEMENT: Spruce like some shade in very hot sun but they will thrive in full sun.

PRUNING AND PINCHING: Needs regular pinching to develop the dense foliage pads.

Blue cedar *(Cedrus atlantica glauca)*

Height: 26" (66 cm) • Width: 20" (51 cm) • Years in training: 4

DESCRIPTION: Tight glaucous needles, easy to pinch and grow.

WATERING: Once a week in winter or just keep the soil damp; once a day in spring; twice a day in summer; and once a day in autumn.

FREE-DRAINING SOIL: 60 percent grit, 40 percent organic (or 50:50 Akadama and Kureyu).

FEEDING: Nitrogen in spring and low nitrogen in late summer. None in midsummer.

PLACEMENT: Bright sun but shade in midsummer.

PRUNING AND PINCHING: Cut the new growth in late spring.

Maples

Japanese Red maple *(Acer palmatum "Deshojo")*

Height: 22" (56 cm) • Width: 19" (48 cm) • Years in training: 15

See page 84 for more information on maples.

> *The Kashima maple here was originally grown as a single tree 18 years ago. The younger trees were cuttings taken from this first tree 10 years ago and then grafted onto the parent tree. The graft has taken excellently and the clump shows good nebari.*

△ Kashima maple

△ Japanese Red maple

Kashima maple *(Acer palmatum)*

Height: 34" (86 cm) • Width: 28" (71 cm) • Years in training: 17

See page 84 for more information on maples.

Trident maple *(Acer buergerianum)*

Height: 32" (81 cm) • **Width: 29" (74 cm)** • **Years in training: 4**
Width of base: 18" – styled from stump

See page 84 for more information on maples.

Yama-Momji maple *(Acer amoenum "Matsumurae")*

Height: 24" (61 cm) • **Width: 18" (46 cm)** • **Years in training: 16**

See page 84 for more information on maples.

Beech

Common European beech

(Fagus sylvatica)

Height: 40" (102 cm) • Width: 31" (79 cm) • Years in training: 0
Just collected

DESCRIPTION: Gray bark and tendency to good *nebari*, or surface roots. Thick trunks are readily available and many old ones are taken from hedges. Shallow root system. This example has just been collected and grown in a training pot for four years. It is now ready to start balancing out of the foliage and reducing the height.

WATERING: Once a week in winter to just keep the soil slightly damp; once a day in spring; twice to three times a day in summer; and once a day in autumn. Does not like soggy soil. Will suffer root rot if kept wet.

FREE-DRAINING SOIL: 50 percent grit, 50 percent organic; or 50 percent Akadama, 30 percent soilless compost, 20 percent grit.

FEEDING: Nitrogen in spring and low nitrogen in late summer. None in midsummer.

PLACEMENT: Bright area. Some shade in midsummer.

PRUNING AND PINCHING: As leaves start to unfurl, pluck out center of new leaf when you can see the green clearly and before it unfurls 50 percent. This will reduce the leaves and cause second bud development elsewhere on branch. General pruning is carried out in midsummer. Seal all cuts.

◁ A Common European beech in winter

Silver or Japanese beech *(Fagus crenata)*

Height: 30" (76 cm) • Width: 19" (48 cm) • Years in training: 8

DESCRIPTION: Silver bark and tendency to good *nebari*, or surface roots. Shallow root system.

WATERING: Once a week in winter to keep slightly damp; once a day in spring; twice to three times a day in summer; once a day in autumn. Will suffer root rot if kept wet.

FREE-DRAINING SOIL: 40 percent grit, 60 percent organic; or 50 percent Akadama, 30 percent soilless compost, 20 percent grit.

FEEDING: Use the following at half-strength—nitrogen in spring and low nitrogen in late summer. None in midsummer.

PLACEMENT: Bright area with some shade in midsummer.

PRUNING AND PINCHING: As leaves start to unfurl, pluck out the center of new leaf when you can see the green clearly and before it unfurls 50 percent. This will reduce the leaves and cause second bud development elsewhere on the branch. General pruning is carried out in midsummer. Seal all cuts. Keep out of frost.

△ Japanese beech, in winter

△ Japanese beech, in fall

Other species

Japanese Kurume azalea

(Rhododendron kiusianum)

**Height: 23" (58 cm) • Width: 20" (51 cm) •
Years in training: 18**

DESCRIPTION: Flowers in fifth or sixth month of season with white, pink, or mixed flowers, late spring to early summer.

WATERING: Once a week in winter to just keep the soil slightly damp; once a day in spring; twice to three times a day in summer; and once a day in autumn.

FREE-DRAINING SOIL: 60 percent grit, 40 percent organic; or 50 percent Kanuma, 30 percent soilless compost, 20 percent grit.

FEEDING: Acid lover. Use Miracid or similar.

PLACEMENT: Keep out of frost.

PRUNING AND PINCHING: After flowering. Pot at that time, too.

1 This azalea (*Rhododentron indicum* "Kaho") had been in training for 15 years. It produces large trumpet flowers in soft shades of pink. It is 27 inches (69 cm) high and 25 inches (64 cm) wide

2 Azaleas in flower

Silver birch *(Betula pendula)*

Height: 33" (84 cm) • Width: 22" (56 cm) • Years in training: 12

DESCRIPTION: Oval leaves. Many forms of birch including the well-liked white birch. You care for all forms in virtually the same way.

WATERING: Once a week in winter to just keep the soil slightly damp; once a day in spring; twice to three times a day in summer; and once a day in autumn.

FREE-DRAINING SOIL: 50 percent grit, 50 percent organic; or 50 percent Akadama, 30 percent soilless compost, 20 percent grit.

FEEDING: Nitrogen in spring and low nitrogen in late summer. None in midsummer. To develop the silver bark, carefully remove the peeling bark when it develops and reduce the nitrogen to two applications in the spring at half strength.

PLACEMENT: Bright area, keep away from frost.

PRUNING AND PINCHING: Pinch back to the first set of leaves at the top of the tree and the second set at the sides once in summer. Nip out leaves when soft, leaving the last pair of new leaves. Keep trunk as clear from pruning cuts as possible. Likes a deeper container when young to encourage roots. Broom or formal upright styles are usual for this type of bonsai because of the way it develops the fine twigs.

△ A full-sized white birch

The bark of mature European White birch has a lovely silver appearance. Though heavy feeding is preferable when young, you need to reduce it if you want the silver color. The American Silver birch or Yellow birch (Betula alleghaniensis) is widely spread in the northeastern parts of the USA and southeastern Canada. Other Birches are: Sweet or Black birch (Betula lenta); River birch, also known as the Red birch, (Betula nigra); Water birch (Betula occidentalis); the famous Indian Paperbark birch (Betula papyrifera), which was used to make birch bark canoes; the Weeping or European Weeping birch (Betula pendula); the Gray or White birch (Betula populifolia); and Ashe or Virginia Roundleaf birch (Betula uber).

Chinese elm *(Ulmus parviflora)*

Height: 30" (76 cm) • Width: 27" (69 cm) • Years in training: 8

DESCRIPTION: Planted in a twin trunk style, this planting emulates two old elms on a hilltop. Elms are one of the easiest of trees to grow – you can use cuttings or even seeds. It is better to grow in the garden for speed of growth or, alternatively, in a growing box. That way, you can lift it once a year and prune the roots, straighten them out and let the leader grow wild. The straightening is particularly important because the trunk needs to be kept as clear of foliage as possible. The beauty is not only in the dense foliage but in the bark. I grew the tall one from seed and the shorter one from a cutting. Both took eight years to get to this stage.

WATERING: Once a week in winter or just keep the soil damp; once a day in spring; twice a day in summer; and once a day in autumn.

FREE-DRAINING SOIL: 60 percent grit, 40 percent organic (or 50:50 Akadama and Kureyu).

FEEDING: Nitrogen in spring and low nitrogen in late summer. None in midsummer.

PLACEMENT: Keep out of frost. Can be kept indoors if grown in a warm area.

PRUNING AND PINCHING: Pinch back to the first set of leaves at the top of the tree and the second set at the sides. Keep the trunk as clear from pruning cuts as possible. Likes a deeper container when young to encourage roots.

△ An elm tree in the wild

Japanese holly *(Ilex crenata)*

**Height: 28" (71 cm) • Width: 29" (74 cm) •
Years in training: 5**

DESCRIPTION: Small, very slightly serrated
leaves with black berries in winter.
There are two forms: male and female.
One is needed to pollinate the other
and then the female will produce
berries. This young tree was trained
from a seedling.

WATERING: Just keep the soil slightly damp
if necessary; once a day in spring; twice
to three times a day in summer; and
once a day in autumn.

FREE-DRAINING SOIL: 50 percent grit,
50 percent organic; or 50 percent
Akadama, 30 percent soilless compost,
20 percent grit.

FEEDING: Nitrogen in spring and low
nitrogen in late summer. None in
midsummer.

PLACEMENT: Indoors or outdoors
depending on climate. Can take slight
shade so is fine for indoors. Keep out
of frost.

PRUNING AND PINCHING: Can be
pruned like a hedge.

Small-leaved lime *(Tilia cordata)*

Height: 22" (56 cm) • Width: 18" (46 cm) • Years in training: 9

WATERING: Once a week in winter to keep the soil slightly damp; once a day in spring; twice to three times a day in summer; and once a day in autumn.

FREE-DRAINING SOIL: 70 percent grit, 30 percent organic or 60 percent Akadama, 20 percent soilless compost, 20 percent grit.

FEEDING: Half-strength through the growing season, every two weeks.

PLACEMENT: Full sun or part shade.

PRUNING AND PINCHING: Light pruning over a few weeks and constant trimming. Wire to shape. Keep trunk clean.

> *In South Carolina, Georgia and North Florida there is a Sour Tupelo lime or Ogeechee Tupelo lime (Nyssa ogeche) and in Central and South Florida and South Texas through to New Mexico, there is another small tree known as the Wild lime or Prickly Ash lime (Zanthoxylum fagara)*

Hawthorn *(Crataegus monogyna)*

Height: 50" (127 cm) • Width: 32" (80 cm) • Years in training: 3

DESCRIPTION: The various species of *Crataegus* are characterized by thorns, stiff wood, and small leaves. They have the benefit of flowers in spring, which are red, white, or pink. This tree is developing its foliage mass and should be completed within another five years.

WATERING: Once a week in winter to keep the soil slightly damp; once a day in spring; twice to three times a day in summer; and once a day in autumn.

FREE-DRAINING SOIL: 50 percent grit, 50 percent organic or 50 percent Akadama, soilless compost 30 percent grit, 20 percent,

FEEDING: Nitrogen in spring and low nitrogen in late summer. None in midsummer.

PLACEMENT: Anywhere, but likes some sun.

PRUNING AND PINCHING: Tends to grow dense, so will need thinning.

△ A hawthorn in a park in Dublin

▷ This large hawthorn is 50 inches (127 cm) high and has been in training for three years since being collected from a hedge. It was chosen for its taper and wide base

Korean hornbeam

(Carpinus coreana)

Height: 28" (71 cm) • Width: 18" (46 cm) •
Years in training: 22

DESCRIPTION: Long oval leaves with serrated
edge. Soft dark stripes on gray trunk. The
tree was originally chopped from a larger
field grown tree and did not grow back
well, so a new leader was grown from the
buds that surrounded the chopped apex.
The tree however is well designed and
when in leaf looks very acceptable and
has great presence.

WATERING: Once a week in winter to just keep
the soil slightly damp; once a day in spring;
twice to three times a day in summer; and
once a day in autumn.

FREE-DRAINING SOIL: 50 percent grit, 50
percent organic; or 50 percent Akadama, 30
percent soilless compost, 20 percent grit.

FEEDING: Nitrogen in spring and low nitrogen
in late summer. None in midsummer.

PLACEMENT: Keep out of frost.

PRUNING AND PINCHING: Pinch back to first
set of leaves at top of the tree and second
set at the sides. Keep trunk as clear from
pruning cuts as possible. Likes a deeper
container when young to encourage roots.

English oak *(Quercus robur)*

Height: 22" (56 cm) • Width: 22" (56 cm) •
Years in training: 6

DESCRIPTION: There are many forms of *Quercus,* such as *cerris, alba,* and *petraea.* Some are smooth-barked and others very corky. Corky barks come from the hotter areas such as southern climates in the northern hemisphere. They can be deciduous or evergreen.

WATERING: Once a week in winter to just keep the soil slightly damp; once a day in spring; twice to three times a day in summer; and once a day in autumn.

FREE-DRAINING SOIL: 50 percent grit, 50 percent organic; or 50 percent Akadama, 30 percent soilless compost, 20 percent grit.

FEEDING: Throughout growing season, a balanced feed like Miracle Grow.

PLACEMENT: Anywhere, but some shade in hot summers to protect pot. Protect from frost.

PRUNING AND PINCHING: Cut back to second set of leaves when young to encourage dichotomous growth. Wire to shape the image. Nip out tips of new shoots after they grow a little to encourage secondary growth. Prune heavy branches. Seal cuts.

◁ An old oak tree in the wild
▽ An English oak in winter

Olive *(Olea europea)*

Height: 24" (61 cm) • Width: 34" (86 cm) • Years in training: 4

DESCRIPTION: Mottled gray or brown bark; heavy trunk can soon develop. Oval glossy leaves. This example was developed from collected material. These were originally two separate bonsai but they were planted together to form a more structured image that will allow branch development over the next three years.

WATERING: Once a week in winter to just keep the soil slightly damp; once a day in spring; twice to three times a day in summer; and once a day in autumn.

FREE-DRAINING SOIL: 70 percent grit, 30 percent organic; or 60 percent Akadama, 20 percent soilless compost, 20 percent grit.

FEEDING: Half-strength through growing season every two weeks.

PLACEMENT: Keep out of frost.

PRUNING AND PINCHING: Light pruning over a few weeks. Wire to shape but be careful wire does not dig in. Keep trunk clean.

△ **An olive tree in a park**

Common privet *(Ligustrum vulgare)*

Height: 15" (38 cm) • Width: 13" (33 cm) • Years in training: 15

WATERING: Once a week in winter to just keep the soil slightly damp; once a day in spring; twice to three times a day in summer; and once a day in autumn.

FREE-DRAINING SOIL: 70 percent grit, 30 percent organic; or 60 percent Akadama, 20 percent soilless compost, 20 percent grit.

FEEDING: Half-strength through growing season every two weeks.

PLACEMENT: Keep out of frost.

PRUNING AND PINCHING: Light pruning over a few weeks. Wire to shape but be careful wire does not dig in. Keep trunk clean. Remove flowers to develop leaves.

Cascade style ▷

I started this tree from a very small bonsai given to me 15 years ago. I liked the gnarled roots, so placed these on a rock to form a rock clasping style. The main branch was left to grow to give strength to the tree but took over the style and before too long I had a kengai or cascade. A very good species for bonsai, it is part of the Olive family. In North America there are a number of trees and shrubs called privet which are also in the Olive family. These include Fringetree or Old man's beard (Chionanthus virginicus), Swamp privet (Texas foresteria) or Adelia (Foresteria acuminate), Florida privet, Florida foresteria, or Wild olive, (Foresteria segregate), White ash (Fraxinus americana), Berlandier or Mexican ash (Fraxinus berlandierana), Carolina (Fraxinus caroliniana), Black, Basket, or Hoop ash (Fraxinus nigra), Green, or Water ash (Fraxinus pennsylvanica), Pumpkin or Red ash (Fraxinus profunda), Texas ash (Fraxinus texensis) and an introduced species, the Chinese privet (Ligustrum sinense). Prune two or three times in the year like a hedge to shape. Develop branches by wiring, but watch for fast growth.

Chinese privet *(Ligustrum sinense)*

Height: 42" (107 cm) • Width: 28" (71 cm) • Years in training: 8

DESCRIPTION: This was cut down from collected material. A
nice foliage mass has been formed and this allows the artist
to develop this image further.

WATERING: Once a week in winter to just keep the soil slightly
damp; once a day in spring; twice to three times a day in
summer; and once a day in autumn.

FREE-DRAINING SOIL: 40 percent grit, 60 percent organic;
or 40 percent Akadama, 40 percent soilless compost,
20 percent grit. Repot every year when young and every
two years until developed. Then every two or three years.
Trim back roots to encourage fine ones, and stop heavy
roots forming.

FEEDING: Very heavy feeder. Full-strength every week through
growing season.

PLACEMENT: Full sun.

PRUNING AND PINCHING: Trim new growth like a hedge and
cut flowers, because these stop the foliage from developing.

Flowering snowbell *(Styrax japonica)*

Height: 32" (81 cm) • Width: 20" (51 cm) • Years in training: 8

DESCRIPTION: Lime-hating like *Stewartia* (see opposite).
Beautiful trunk pattern of light gray with darker markings.
Lovely flowers in spring. This tree was cut from a larger tree
and a new apex is being formed. The new wavy apex will be

◁ Flowering snowbell

reduced as the branches develop at the base of this area, and the apex will be tightened down to the original height, which will help form a much more balanced, stronger image.

WATERING: Once a week in winter to keep the soil slightly damp; once a day in spring; twice to three times a day in summer; and once a day in autumn.

FREE-DRAINING SOIL: Lime-free—50 percent grit, 50 percent organic; or 50 percent Akadama, 30 percent lime-free soilless compost, 20 percent grit.

FEEDING: Every two weeks through growing season with Miracid.

PLACEMENT: Keep out of frost. Likes full sun.

PRUNING AND PINCHING: Pinch new growth through the growing season.

Stewartia *(Stewartia monadelpha)*

Height: 22" (56 cm) • Width: 14" (36 cm) • Years in training: 10

WATERING: Use soft water only. Once a week in winter; to keep the soil slightly damp; once a day in spring; twice to three times a day in summer; and once a day in autumn.

FREE-DRAINING SOIL: 50 percent grit, 50 percent organic; or 50 percent Akadama, 30 percent soilless compost, 20 percent grit, all lime-free.

FEEDING: For acid-loving plants.

PLACEMENT: Keep out of frost. Part-shade but bring out to full sun in spring and autumn to develop the bark and orange color that epitomizes this tree.

PRUNING AND PINCHING: Cut back to the second or third set of leaves and try to develop the upward appearance of the bonsai.

This tree was initially trained incorrectly, as the previous owner tried to bend the normally upward growing branches into a downward shape. It is much easier to either train them straight or slightly elevated. Unfortunately the apex is damaged and the sides will need to be kept shorter as this tree is side-dominant and therefore weaker at the apex. This tree will be styled as an individual slanting style bonsai.

△ Stewartia

Websites and Magazines

www.bonsaiinformation.co.uk

Information only and not a site where you can ask questions. There are links to a number of worldwide sources of good information such as clubs and magazines, and also Craig Hunt's site. This site introduces the Internet Bonsai Club, the various collections of bonsai, and most of the dealers around the globe. Lecture and convention bookings can be made by contacting: craig@bonsaiinformation.co.uk or craig.coussins@btinternet.com

I suggest that if you really wish to learn then you will need to invest in all three of the following excellent magazines, because each is exceptional its own way. You will find a selection of dealers around Europe, America, and Canada who are bonsai specialists.

- Bonsai Today – (www.stonelantern.com)
  The premier Japanese publication translated into English and published in America by John Palmer for the intermediate to advanced enthusiasts. Back issues are available from:
    Stone Lantern Publishing Company
    PO Box 816 Sudbury
    Massachusetts
    MA 01776, U.S.A.

- Bonsai Magazine – (www.bonsaimagazine.com)
  The European English-language magazine featuring many of the top European artists. Edited by the well-known European master, Farrand Bloch. Back issues are available from:
    P.O. Box 17
    4040 DA Kesteren
    The Netherlands
    Tel: 011-31 488 443993 from North America;
    + 31 (0) 488 443993 elsewhere.
    Fax: 011-31-488 443861
    Email: info@bonsaimagazine.nl
    for Farrand Bloch (editor): editor@bonsaimagazine.nl
    Sales: sales@bonsaimagazine.nl

- International Bonsai – (www.internationalbonsai.com)
  One of the finest of the bonsai magazines. The bonsai master William Valavanis looks at work from all over the Americas as well as the Far East. Back issues are available from:
    The International Bonsai Arboretum
    William Valavanis
    P.O. Box 23894
    Rochester
    New York 14692-3894
    U.S.A.

- Bonsai Clubs International – (www.bonsai-bci.com)
  BCI produce a magazine, editor Donna Banting. It is well worth reading, because it covers many beginner-to-intermediate articles with input from the world's top bonsai artists and masters. It details where you can find a local bonsai club. You can join BCI, too, or just search through the excellent website.

Acknowledgments

My thanks go to the following people:

Toria Leitch and staff of Quintet for being understanding and supportive.

My wife Svetlana, who was missed over many days and nights while I was writing this book, and who kept me supplied with tea, food, and lots of love.

Four excellent bonsai artists who helped me throughout the process: Kevin Bailey, who not only edited the technical text for me but helped me with styling photographs; Alan Dorling, Peter Snart, and Robert Porch, who also helped with styling photographs; and Jean Snart, who made sure we were fed and watered throughout.

Willowbog Bonsai Centre, Hexham, England.

Mike Box, Len Gilbert, Steve Cousins and many other friends.

Four bonsai masters who taught me American bonsai: Gary Marchal of New Orleans for letting me photograph his magnificent Bald cypress collection, and who took me through the swamps of Louisiana; Joe Day and my friends in Alabama who kindly contributed to this book; and Ed Trout and Mary Madison for teaching me about Florida bonsai.

Picture credits

Bill Jordan, photographs of pests and diseases featured on pages 50-53.

Salvatore Liporace, images featured on pages 14, 15, 16, 17(4), 60 and 61.

Jacqui Hurst, The Garden Picture Library page 13, 22

Elizabeth Whiting Associates page 38

Craig Coussins: pages 9, 10/11, 12, 16/17(1,2,3), 18/19. 23, 26/27, 32, 37, 40/41, 43, 44/45, 54/55, 56, 62/63, 64/65, 66, 71(bottom), 72, 73(middle and bottom), 74/75, 78, 79(bottom), 82/83, 85, 115(bottom), 116(bottom), 118(bottom), 121(top)

Quintet Publishing Ltd, pages 20, 25, 28/29, 31, 42, 46/47, 48, 57, 58, 59, 67, 68/69, 70, 71(top & middle), 73(top), 76/77, 79(top right), 81, 84, 86-125

Page numbers in *italic* type refer to picture captions.